WORDS FOR ALL SEASONS

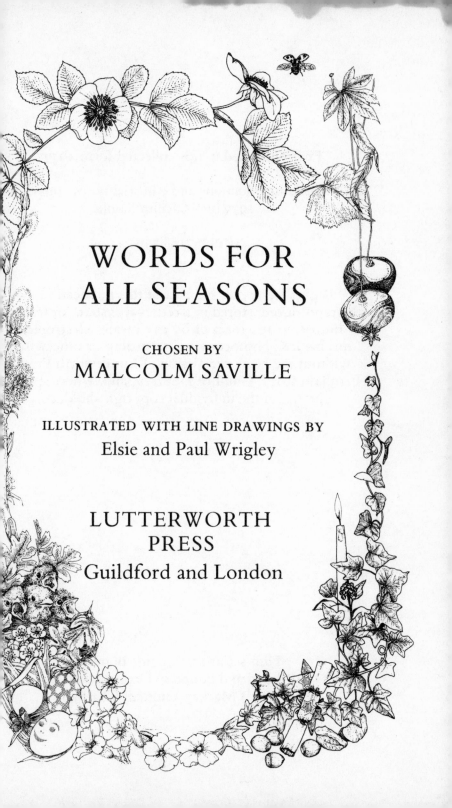

WORDS FOR ALL SEASONS

CHOSEN BY
MALCOLM SAVILLE

ILLUSTRATED WITH LINE DRAWINGS BY
Elsie and Paul Wrigley

LUTTERWORTH PRESS
Guildford and London

Film set in 12/13 point Bembo
Printed and bound in Great Britain
by W & J Mackay Limited, Chatham

TO MY WIFE

Perceiv'st thou not the process of the year,
How the four seasons in four forms appear
Resembling Human Life in every shape and wear?

William Shakespeare

Contents

Note

Some of the poems and verses used in this book are very old – so old that no one now knows who wrote them. They are often said to be 'Anon.' (anonymous) or 'Trad.' (traditional). In this book they appear without any author's name below them. There are also one or two poems, such as *Summer is Nigh* on page 74, where no name is given because my publishers and I have been unable to discover their authors. We would welcome the opportunity to insert proper acknowledgment for these in any future edition of this book.

There is a list of copyright acknowledgments on page 186. If we have inadvertently infringed any copyright, we would be glad to set the matter right in any future edition, and to pay the customary fee, at the current recommended Society of Authors rate.

The titles of the poems in this book are generally, but not always, those given by the authors. Sometimes, however, I have inserted a different title, either to carry forward the theme of the seasons which runs through this book, or, more frequently, because I am only using an extract from a longer piece. Most of the titles printed in inverted commas have been supplied by me in this way.

The title of the book itself, *Words for all Seasons,* was suggested by a phrase which a man called Robert Whittinton used of the great Sir Thomas More, his contemporary. He said of More: that he was 'as tyme requyreth, a man of marveylous myrth and pastymes, & somtyme of as sad gravyte, as who say a man for all seasons'. So, for me, are the passages and poems quoted in this book.

Acknowledgments

I have many to thank for the help given to me in the making of this book. First, my wife and family, including ten of my twelve grandchildren – the last two being only at the beginning of their journey through the seasons. I owe much to many friends and wish to acknowledge practical and professional help from Richard Henwood, whose belief in the concept of this book has never wavered. Also to my Editor, Jenny Overton, who has introduced me to the work of modern poets, some examples of which have enriched these pages.

Last, but certainly not least, I am grateful to a hundred faithful readers of my other books to whom I wrote asking for their favourite choice of poems and stories. Although I have not been able to use all their suggestions, my final selection owes much to their interest in the project and their loyalty to me.

M.S.

Four seasons fill the measure of the year;
There are four seasons in the mind of man:
He has his lusty spring, when fancy clear
Takes in all beauty with an easy span:
He has his summer, when luxuriously
Spring's honey'd cud of youthful thought he loves
To ruminate, and by such dreaming nigh
His nearest unto heaven: quiet coves
His soul has in its autumn, when his wings
He furleth close; contented so to look
On mists in idleness – to let fair things
Pass by unheeded as a threshold brook:
He has his winter too of pale misfeature,
Or else he would forego his mortal nature.

John Keats

Foreword

This book, for me, is a dream come true. Although I have written many books, it has always been my ambition to make a book of what other writers and poets have contributed for other generations than their own. Of words left, not only for the inspiration of the young, but for all to whom childhood, youth and family life, are important.

Words are my business and my delight. In these pages I hope to share with all readers, whatever their age, words which have enriched my life, strengthened my belief in childhood and youth, and rekindled my faith in the eternal verities based, for me, on Christianity.

There is nothing in this book which I do not admire and am not happy to remember. Although I owe much to many helpers and friends, the final choice is mine.

The plan is simple. Indeed it is basic, because the pattern of all our lives follows the unchanging rhythm of the seasons. In the Spring the world is renewed and when a baby is born a new life begins. Summer is the time of growth as Nature prepares for harvest, and so our lives and personalities mature as we leave childhood behind. Autumn has been called the crown of the year, but perhaps fulfilment is a better word. And so with us. The crown of our years is when we fulfil ourselves as men and women. In Winter the natural world sleeps, but it is Shelley, one of the greatest of British poets, who reminds us that 'If Winter comes, can Spring be far behind?'

We can all accept that the pageant of the seasons matches our lives from birth to death. Christians believe that this is God's plan, and it is a fact that the great

Festivals of the Church deliberately remind us of this pattern. Easter and the joy of Resurrection come with the daffodils, and when the days are shortest and perhaps remind us of old age, comes the miracle of Christmas, the most wonderful of all births.

The book has been planned to be read straight through rather than dipped into, but I have deliberately chosen some poems for the youngest, and some of these are remembered from my own childhood and still enjoyed today by my youngest grandchildren. Some of the other selections are more difficult and subtle – but so is life!

I hope this book will bring to all my readers many joys, happy remembrances, and much gratitude to those who have left for us so many imperishable words for all seasons.

Chelsea Cottage,
Winchelsea,
East Sussex.

14

Spring
of
Youth

For, lo, the winter is past,
The rain is over and gone;
The flowers appear on the earth;
The time of the singing of birds is come.

Spring often comes with hurrying feet. Suddenly there is a day when our own gentle West wind clears the skies. The sun warms the new-born lambs and calls us out to greet the miracle of another year.

That is why, in this first section, I have chosen many poems about this wonderful awakening – of flowers and hedgerows and garden surprises, and, of course, of birds because this is the season when our visitors cross the sea to come back to us. And because these are the days of youth, some of the verses have been chosen for younger readers and have reminded me how much I loved them in my childhood – some almost before I could read them myself.

I hope you will smile at *If You Were a Flower* which was written by a friend who loved gardens. Another old comrade contributes *Innocence* on page 61. Please enjoy it as much as I do. I do not think that you will guess that *Groveley Wood in March* was written by a working farmer, but I have included it because if you read it carefully you can almost hear the birds singing!

Because I was born in Sussex and still live there, I had to offer you *Swallows over the South Downs* which is one of my favourites. These tiny, fearless messengers of Spring come to us in April, usually a few days before we hear the first cuckoo.

But the heart of Spring is surely Easter, the greatest of Christian Festivals. Resurrection means 'restoring to life' as I have tried to emphasise in most of my Spring selections. But there is no Easter without Good Friday and before that is Palm Sunday, preceded by the penitent days of Lent, which begins with Ash Wednesday.

I hope you will enjoy *Jack o' Lent* as a reminder of Ash Wednesday. My Editor's introduction to this poem was one of my happiest surprises, which I want to share with you.

Now fades the last long streak of snow,
Now burgeons every maze of quick
About the flowering squares, and thick
By ashen roots the violets blow.

Alfred, Lord Tennyson

'To Welcome in the Year'

Little Boy
Full of joy.
Little Girl
Sweet and small,
Cock does crow
So do you.
Merry voice
Infant noise
Merrily Merrily to welcome in the Year

William Blake
from Spring

'A New-Born Child'

The baby would come soon, the nurse told everybody. There was no chance to get to the doctor through the drifts, but she could manage. There was food in the larder, baskets of eggs which could not go to the dealers, butter made from the new milk, cheeses, home-baked bread and a sack of flour ready for more bread, and a side of bacon. No one would starve. Onions, apples, carrots, potatoes were stored ready for winter, and the sugar jar was full to the brim with fifty pounds of brown sugar.

Fires were heaped with wood and coal, wood from the store in the barn, coal from the great open coal-place, where the ivy tods leaned over the walls. Everybody who entered the house stamped their feet to rid them of the snow, and the fires crackled and roared in the frosty air. Water was carried from the troughs each day after Willie and my father had broken the ice with axe-heads. Patty filled the shining cans with the sweet spring water, which looked black under the ice. Copper kettles were boiled and the large copper pan was ready with hot water for any emergencies.

So I was born in this wild storm, with deep snow on the ground, and cattle shut in their houses, and horses in the stable. I was bathed in spring water heated over the fire, and I was held up to the window to open my eyes and look out over the fields at the dazzling whiteness, and to look at the candles in their brass candlesticks, alight to welcome me.

After a few days I was taken downstairs, but first the nurse carried me in my long robe and shawl up the stairs to the attic. That was a tradition.

'A new-born child must always be taken up before it goes down, so it will go up in life and not down'. . . .

I was wrapped in the long flannel nightdress over the thin lawn nightgown that babies wore, and laid in a drawer to sleep. There was no cradle, and the green wooden crib provided for me was too big for a baby. The old nurse took the deepest drawer from the polished mahogany chest of drawers, and lined it with blankets. She laid the drawer across two chairs and behold, a lovely cot for me.

The first flowers I saw were snowdrops from the orchard, picked to give my mother pleasure. . . . The first stars I saw were the winter stars shining in the great dome of the sky. I was taken out in my mother's arms wrapped closely in a shawl to see the moon and stars, and to hear the lullaby sung to me:

> 'Twinkle, twinkle, little star,
> How I wonder what you are?
> Up above the world so high,
> Like a diamond in the sky.'

Alison Uttley
from The Snow-baby, *in* A Peck of Gold

'Star Wish'

Star light, star bright,
First star I see tonight,
I wish I may, I wish I might,
Have the wish I wish tonight.

'Moon Blessing'

I see the moon
And the moon sees me,
God bless the priest
That christened me.

'Carol for St Valentine's'

St Valentine, that art full high aloft,
Thus sing the little birds all for thy sake:

'Now welcome, Summer, with thy sun so soft,
That hast this winter's weathers made to shake.'

Well have they cause, so to sing gladly oft,
Since each of them recovered hath his mate:

'Now welcome, Summer, with thy sun so soft,
That hast this winter's weathers made to shake.'

Full blissful may they sing when they do wake:

'Now welcome, Summer, with thy sun so soft,
That hast this winter's weathers made to shake,
And the nights long and black hath driven off.'

The carol is based on the old belief that the birds choose their
mates on St Valentine's Day. It has been freely adapted from
a poem written by Geoffrey Chaucer some 600 years ago, at
the end of his long narrative poem, *The Parliament of Fowls.*

'Hail, Bishop Valentine'

Hail Bishop Valentine, whose day this is,
    All the Air is thy Diocese,
    And all the chirping Choristers
And other birds are thy Parishioners,
    Thou marriest every year
The lyric Lark, and the grave whispering Dove,
The Sparrow that neglects his life for love,
The household Bird, with the red stomacher. . . .

John Donne
from an Epithalamion

'Valentine for a Mother'

More shower than shine
Brings sweet St Valentine;
Warm shine, warm shower,
Bring up sweet flower on flower.

Through shower and shine
Loves you your Valentine,
Through shine, through shower,
Through summer's flush,
Through autumn's fading hour.

Christina Rossetti

'Green of Spring'

Every valley drinks,
Every dell and hollow;
Where the kind rain sinks and sinks,
Green of Spring will follow.

Yet a lapse of weeks —
Buds will burst their edges,
Strip their wool-coats, glue-coats, streaks
In the woods and hedges;

Weave a bower of love
For birds to meet each other,
Weave a canopy above
Nest and egg and mother.

Christina Rossetti
from Winter Rain

Shrove Tuesday: Pancake Day

The Pancake

Mix a pancake,
Stir a pancake,
Pop it in the pan.

Fry the pancake,
Toss the pancake,
Catch it if you can.

Christina Rossetti

Ash Wednesday

Jack o' Lent

Where are you running to, Jack o' Lent,
Your yellow coat so ruined and rent?
I'm going to the sea-shore as fast as I can
To try and find the Galilee man.

What will you have from him, Jack o' Lent,
Before your thirty of silver is spent?
I'll have some fish and I'll have some bread
And some words to cure the pain in my head.

How long will it take you, Jack o' Lent,
Your legs all crooked, your body all bent?
With the help of prayer and the help of praise
It'll take me forty nights and days.

Should you not find him, Jack o' Lent,
What will then be your intent?
I'll find the hungry and find the poor
And scatter my silver at their door.

What will you do then, Jack o' Lent,
If nobody takes a single cent?
I'll go to the rope-maker cunning and old
And buy me a collar against the cold.

Where will your lodging be, Jack o' Lent,
If house and home give no content?
I'll climb as high as heaven's hem
And take my rest on a sycamore stem.

What can we do for you, Jack o' Lent,
If in the fire the tree is pent?
  Take the fire and take the flame
  And burn the curse from off my name.

What shall we do then, Jack o' Lent,
If all to ashes you are sent?
  Take the cinders you can see.
  Cross your brow. Remember me.

Charles Causley

In Cornwall, figures representing Judas Iscariot, and called
'Jack o' Lent's', used to be paraded round towns and villages
on Ash Wednesday and later burnt on bonfires.

29

White Lent

Now quit your care
And anxious fear and worry;
For schemes are vain
And fretting brings no gain.
To prayer, to prayer!
Bells call and clash and hurry,
In Lent the bells do cry,
'Come buy, come buy,
Come buy with love the love most high!'

Lent comes in the Spring,
And Spring is pied with brightness;
The sweetest flowers,
Keen winds, and sun, and showers,
Their health do bring
To make Lent's chastened whiteness;
For life to men brings light
And might, and might,
And might to those whose hearts are right.

To bow the head
In sackcloth and in ashes,
Or rend the soul,
Such grief is not Lent's goal;
But to be led
To where God's glory flashes,
His beauty to come nigh,
To fly, to fly,
To fly where truth and light do lie.

The opening verses of a carol tr. Percy Dearmer

'A Change in the Year'

It is the first mild day of March:
Each minute sweeter than before,
The Redbreast sings from the tall Larch
That stands beside our door.

There is a blessing in the air,
Which seems a sense of joy to yield
To the bare trees, and mountains bare,
And grass in the green field.

William Wordsworth
from a poem
to his sister Dorothy

A March Calf

Right from the start he is dressed in his best –
  his blacks and his whites.
Little Fauntleroy – quiffed and glossy,
A Sunday suit, a wedding natty get-up,
Standing in dunged straw

Under cobwebby beams, near the mud wall,
Half of him legs,
Shining-eyed, requiring nothing more
But that mother's milk come back often.

Everything else is in order, just as it is.
Let the summer skies hold off, for the moment.
This is just as he wants it.
A little at a time, of each new thing, is best.

Too much and too sudden is too frightening –
When I block the light, a bulk from space,
To let him in to his mother for a suck,
He bolts a yard or two, then freezes,

Staring from every hair in all directions,
Ready for the worst, shut up in his hopeful religion,
A little syllogism
With a wet blue-reddish muzzle, for God's thumb.

You see all his hopes bustling
As he reaches between the worn rails towards
The topheavy oven of his mother.
He trembles to grow, stretching his curl-tip tongue –

What did cattle ever find here
To make this dear little fellow
So eager to prepare himself?
He is already in the race, and quivering to win –

His new purpled eyeball swivel-jerks
In the elbowing push of his plans.
Hungry people are getting hungrier,
Butchers developing expertise and markets,

But he just wobbles his tail – and glistens
Within his dapper profile
Unaware of how his whole lineage
Has been tied up.

He shivers for feel of the world licking his side.
He is like an ember – one glow
Of lighting himself up
With the fuel of himself, breathing and brightening.

Soon he'll plunge out, to scatter his seething joy,
To be present at the grass,
To be free on the surface of such a wideness,
To find himself. To stand. To moo.

Ted Hughes

'A-Mothering on Sunday'

It is the day of all the year,
Of all the year the one day,
When I shall see my Mother dear
   And bring her cheer,
A-Mothering on Sunday.

And now to fetch my wheaten cake,
To fetch it from the baker,
He promised me, for Mother's sake,
   The best he'd bake
For me to fetch and take her.

Well have I known, as I went by
One hollow lane, that none day
I'd fail to find – for all they're shy –
   Where violets lie,
As I went home on Sunday.

My sister Jane is waiting-maid
Along with Squire's lady,
And year by year her part she's played,
   And home she stayed
To get the dinner ready.

For Mother'll come to Church, you'll see –
Of all the year it's the day –
'The one,' she'll say, 'that's made for me.'
   And so it be:
It's every Mother's free day.

The boys will all come home from town,
Not one will miss that one day;
And every maid
   will bustle down
    To show her gown,
A-Mothering on Sunday.

It is the day of all the year,
Of all the year the one day;
And here come I,
   my Mother dear,
    To bring you cheer,
A-Mothering on Sunday.

verses from a carol by
George Hare Leonard

On Mothering Sunday, it used to be customary for maids
and apprentices, who seldom had a chance of going home, to
be allowed one day's holiday to visit their parents. They took
gifts with them – simnel cakes, sugar plums, violets – and
then, while one of the daughters cooked the midday dinner,
each mother would have a free day and, for once, the chance
of going to morning service with her children.

The Green Lane

A little lane – the brook runs close beside,
And spangles in the sunshine,
  while the fish glide swiftly by;
And hedges leafing with the green springtide;
From out their greenery the old birds fly,
And chirp and whistle in the morning sun;
The pilewort glitters 'neath the pale blue sky,
The little robin has its nest begun,
And grass-green linnets round the bushes fly.
How mild the spring comes in! the daisy buds
Lift up their golden blossoms to the sky.
How lovely are the pingles and the woods.
Here a beetle runs – and there a fly
Rests on the arum leaf in bottle-green,
And all the spring in this sweet lane is seen.

John Clare

Groveley Wood in March

We rode up through Groveley Wood. At every season of the year this wood is beautiful, but just now it is very lovely indeed. Spring's sudden visit seemed to have caught even the trees unawares, and they are hurrying to catch up with her, or to put it another way, Spring is positively bustling them into their clothes. As we rode I noticed that fresh colour was showing everywhere against the sombre black of their winter nakedness. Green predominated, but the beeches were covered with a pinkish film; here and there a drift of almond-coloured palm showed against a background of dark-green spruce; while around us on every side green honeysuckle twined eagerly amongst the breaking hazel buds.

But the loveliest thing of all was the continuous chorus of the birds. When we entered the wood a pigeon or two clattered noisily away, a blackbird rattled his danger signal, and a jay screamed a hoarse warning of our intrusion. But when we arrived in the middle of the wood we stopped for a few moments to listen, and all around us was song in praise of Spring, sung by an invisible choir – coos, chuckles, chirrupings, baritone from the blackbird, contralto from the thrush, and every now and again a thin treble thread of melody from the smaller songbirds.

A. G. Street
from A Country Calendar

The Annunciation

The angel Gabriel was sent from God to a city of Galilee named Nazareth, to a virgin betrothed to a man whose name was Joseph, of the house of David; and the virgin's name was Mary. And he came to her and said, 'Hail, O favoured one, the Lord is with you!' But she was greatly troubled at the saying, and considered in her mind what sort of greeting this might be. And the angel said to her, 'Do not be afraid, Mary, for you have found favour with God. And behold, you will conceive in your womb and bear a son, and you shall call his name Jesus. He will be great, and will be called the Son of the Most High; and the Lord God will give to him the throne of his father David, and he will reign over the house of Jacob for ever; and of his kingdom there will be no end.'

St Luke, 1, 26–33

Lady Day

Where did Gabriel get a lily,
In the month of March,
    When the green
    Is hardly seen
On the early larch?
    Though I know
    Just where they grow,
I have pulled no daffodilly.
Where did Gabriel get a lily
In the month of March?
    Could I bring
    The tardy spring
Under her foot's arch,
    Near and far,
    The primrose star
Should bloom with violets, willy-nilly.
    Where did Gabriel get a lily
    In the month of March?

G. James

Swallows over the South Downs

England, we're here again,
Sleet-squalls and blinding rain
(All just as usual)
   Greet us on landing.
Head-winds through Italy,
Fog over Brittany,
Why we don't give it up's
   Past understanding.

Buffeted, blown, half-dead . . .
Hey, look, there's Beachy Head!
Green turf and milky-white
   Chalk-cliffs like Dover!
Sun-gleams at last, hurray!
. . . I'm off down Uckfield way,
Country'll be looking grand
   Now the rain's over.

. . . Primroses, blowing leaves,
Thatched roofs and cottage eaves,
Oast-houses, dusky-dark,
   What sites for nesting!
Come on, the fun's begun,
Hurry up, everyone,
Don't let's waste any time
   Preening and resting. . . .

Mary Holden

The Throstle

'Summer is coming, summer is coming,
 I know it, I know it, I know it.
Light again, leaf again, life again, love again,'
 Yes, my wild little Poet.

Sing the new year in under the blue.
 Last year you sang it as gladly.
'New, new, new, new!' Is it then *so* new
 That you should carol so madly?

'Love again, song again, nest again, young again,'
 Never a prophet so crazy!
And hardly a daisy as yet, little friend,
 See, there is hardly a daisy.

'Here again, here, here, here, happy year!'
 O warble unchidden, unbidden!
Summer is coming, is coming, my dear,
 And all the winters are hidden.

Alfred, Lord Tennyson

Two Sparrows

Two sparrows, feeding,
heard a thrush
sing to the dawn,
the first said, 'Tush!

in all my life
I have never heard
a more affected
singing bird.'

The second said,
'It's you and me,
who slave to keep
the likes of he.'

'And if we cared,'
both sparrows said,
'we'd do that singing
on our head.'

The thrush pecked sideways
and was dumb.
'And now,' they screamed,
'he's pinched our crumb!'

Humbert Wolfe

The Woods and Banks

The woods and banks of England now,
  Late coppered with dead leaves and old,
Have made the early violets grow,
  And bulge with knots of primrose gold.
Hear how the blackbird flutes away,
  Whose music scorns to sleep at night:
Hear how the cuckoo shouts all day
  For echoes – to the world's delight:
Hullo, you imp of wonder, you –
  Where are you now, cuckoo? Cuckoo?

W. H. Davies

The Killer Frost

We didn't like the blossom to come too early. In forward seasons the plum orchards would get their first sprinkling of snow at the end of March, with the cherry – 'loveliest of trees' – breaking into full bloom a few days later. The growers would shake their heads gravely. 'Hast seen the blow a-blowin' at Brensham? . . . If we should get two-three sharp frosses now . . . ' That would mean the ruin of their crops – in some cases, where 'little men' depended on a few acres for their livelihood, it might mean their own ruin. They dreaded the brief white frosts of middle spring which crept with the early-morning mists up the valley; but worst of all were hailstorms followed by keen nights:

'If the drop do freeze in the cup of the plum,
We shall have neither cherry nor plum!'

John Moore
from A Portrait of Elmbury

44

Loveliest of Trees

Loveliest of trees, the cherry now
Is hung with bloom along the bough,
And stands about the woodland ride
Wearing white for Eastertide.

Now, of my threescore years and ten,
Twenty will not come again,
And take from seventy springs a score,
It only leaves me fifty more.

And since to look at things in bloom
Fifty springs are little room,
About the woodlands I will go
To see the cherry hung with snow.

A. E. Housman

The Cherry Trees

The cherry trees bend over and are shedding
On the old road where all that passed are dead,
Their petals, strewing the grass as for a wedding
This early May morn when there is none to wed.

Edward Thomas

The Donkey

I saw a donkey
One day old,
His head was too big
For his neck to hold:
His legs were shaky
And long and loose,
They rocked and staggered
And weren't much use.

He tried to gambol
And frisk a bit,
But he wasn't quite sure
Of the trick of it.
His queer little coat
Was soft and grey,
And curled at his neck
In a lovely way.

His face was wistful
And left no doubt
That he felt life needed
Some thinking about.
So he blundered round
In venturesome quest,
And then lay flat
On the ground to rest.
He looked so little
And weak and slim,
I prayed the world
Might be good to him.

Gertrude Hind

Young Lambs

The spring is coming by a-many signs;
  The trays are up, the hedges broken down,
  That fenced the haystack, and the remnant shines
  Like some old antique fragment weathered brown.
And where suns peep, in every sheltered place,
  The little early buttercups unfold
A glittering star or two – till many trace
  The edges of the blackthorn clumps in gold.
And then a little lamb bolts up behind
  The hill and wags his tail to meet the yoe,
And then another, sheltered from the wind,
  Lies all his length as dead – and lets me go
Close by and never stirs but baking lies,
With legs stretched out as though he could not rise.

John Clare

The Lamb

　　Little Lamb who made thee?
　　Dost thou know who made thee?
Gave thee life and bid thee feed
By the stream and o'er the mead;
Gave thee clothing of delight,
Softest clothing woolly bright;
Gave thee such a tender voice,
Making all the vales rejoice:
　　Little Lamb who made thee?
　　Dost thou know who made thee?

　　Little Lamb I'll tell thee,
　　Little Lamb I'll tell thee:
He is called by thy name,
For he calls himself a Lamb:
He is meek and he is mild,
He became a little child:
I a child and thou a lamb,
We are called by his name.
　　Little Lamb God bless thee.
　　Little Lamb God bless thee.

William Blake

49

Green Rain

Into the scented woods we'll go
And see the blackthorn swim in snow.
High above, in the budding leaves,
A brooding dove awakes and grieves;
The glades with mingled music stir,
And wildly laughs the woodpecker.
When blackthorn petals pearl the breeze,
There are the twisted hawthorn trees
Thick-set with buds, as clear and pale
As golden water or green hail –
As if a storm of rain had stood
Enchanted in the thorny wood,
And, hearing fairy voices call,
Hung poised, forgetting how to fall.

Mary Webb

The Lent Lily

'Tis spring; come out to ramble
  The hilly brakes around,
For under thorn and bramble
  About the hollow ground
  The primroses are found.

And there's the windflower chilly
  With all the winds at play,
And there's the Lenten lily
  That has not long to stay
  And dies on Easter Day.

And since till girls go maying
  You find the primrose still,
And find the windflower playing
  With every wind at will,
  But not the daffodil,

Bring baskets now, and sally
  Upon the spring's array,
And bear from hill and valley
  The daffodil away
  That dies on Easter Day.

A. E. Housman

The Donkey

When fishes flew and forests walked
    And figs grew upon thorn,
Some moment when the moon was blood
    Then surely I was born.

With monstrous head and sickening cry
    And ears like errant wings,
The devil's walking parody
    Of all four-footed things.

The tattered outlaw of the earth,
    Of ancient crooked will;
Starve, scourge, deride me: I am dumb,
    I keep my secret still.

Fools! For I also had my hour;
    One far fierce hour and sweet:
There was a shout about my ears,
    And palms before my feet.

G. K. Chesterton

The Wood Fire

'This is a brightsome blaze you've lit, good friend, tonight!'

'Aye, it has been the bleakest spring I have felt for years,
And nought compares with cloven logs to keep alight:
I buy them bargain-cheap of the executioners,
As I dwell near; and they wanted the crosses out of sight
By Passover, not to affront the eyes of visitors.

Yes, they're from the crucifixions last week-ending
At Kranion. We can sometimes use the poles again,
But they get split by the nails, and 'tis quicker work
                                        than mending
To knock together new; though the uprights now and then
Serve twice when they're let stand. But if a feast's
                                        impending,
As lately, you've to tidy up for the comers' ken.

Though only three were impaled, you may know it
                                        didn't pass off
So quietly as was wont? That Galilee carpenter's son
Who boasted he was king, incensed the rabble to scoff:
I heard the noise from my garden. This piece is the
                                        one he was on . . .
Yes, it blazes up well if lit with a few dry chips and shroff;
And it's worthless for much else, what with cuts and
                                        stains thereon.'

Thomas Hardy

53

Easter Night

All night had shout of men and cry
Of woeful women filled his way;
Until that noon of sombre sky
On Friday, clamour and display
Smote him; no solitude had he,
No silence, since Gethsemene.

Public was Death; but Power, but Might,
But Life again, but Victory,
Were hushed within the dead of night,
The shuttered dark, the secrecy,
And all alone, alone, alone
He rose again behind the stone.

Alice Meynell

Easter's Flowers

What profusion is offered! Primrose, moody violet, and up-thrusting potent crocus: daffodil and the more magic wild daffodil: hyacinth and grape hyacinth: windflowers like an exercise in delicacy and the anemones of the Holy Land believed to be 'the lilies of the field': squills and jonquils and the pasque flower; crooked blackthorn glorified, Star of Bethlehem, flowering currant in a cloud of tingling fragrance, apple blow and wild cherry; childish periwinkle and cuckoo-point; and, for a very late Easter, speedwell and the gold-tasselled trophies of the oak.

Laurence Whistler

'It is now Easter'

It is now Easter, and Jack of Lent is turned out of doors. . . . The air is wholesome and the sky comfortable, the flowers odoriferous and the fruits pleasant. I conclude, it is a day of much delightfulness: the sun's dancing day, and the earth's holy-day.

Nicholas Breton
from Fantastickes

'I Watched a Blackbird'

I watched a blackbird on a budding sycamore
One Easter Day, when sap was stirring twigs to the cor
   I saw his tongue, and crocus-coloured bill
   Parting and closing as he turned his trill;
   Then he flew down, seized on a stem of hay,
And upped to where his building scheme was under wa
As if so sure a nest were never shaped on spray.

Thomas Ha

Rhyme

Hear what the mournful linnets say:
   'We built our nest compact and warm,
But cruel boys came round our way
   And took our summerhouse by storm.

They crushed the eggs so neatly laid;
   So now we sit with drooping wing,
And watch the ruin they have made,
   Too late to build, too sad to sing.'

Christina Rossetti

'Spring is Come Home'

. . . For lo, into her house
Spring is come home with her world-wandering feet,
And all things are made young with young desires;
And all for her is light increased
In yellow stars and yellow daffodils. . . .

Francis Thompson
from An Ode after Easter

'Daffodils so Beautiful'

April 15, 1802: Grasmere, in the Lake District

It was a threatening, misty morning, but mild. We set off after dinner from Eusemere. . . . A few primroses by the roadside – woodsorrel flower, the anemone, scentless violets, strawberries, and that starry yellow flower which Mrs C [Mrs Coleridge] calls pilewort. When we were in the woods beyond Gowbarrow Park we saw a few daffodils close to the water-side. We fancied that the lake had floated the seeds ashore, and that the little colony had so sprung up. But as we went along there were more and yet more; and at last, under the boughs of the trees, we saw that there was a long belt of them along the shore, about the breadth of a country turnpike road. I never saw daffodils so beautiful. They grew among the mossy stones about and about them; some rested their heads upon these stones as on a pillow for weariness; and the rest tossed and reeled and danced, and seemed as if they verily laughed with the wind, that blew upon them over the lake; they looked so gay, ever dancing, ever changing.

Dorothy Wordsworth
from her Journal

If you were a Flower

Don't be a snowdrop:
　It wouldn't be nice
To sleep in the snow
　On a mattress of ice.

Don't be a tulip,
　So tall and erect:
All looking alike
　And so very correct.

Don't be a bluebell:
　Though charmed by your grace,
Trippers will strew you
　All over the place.

Just be an orchid:
　If you take my advice
You'll be ever so rich
　And look ever so nice.

Reginald Arkell

Innocence

Lord, I have often wondered why
So many stars are in the sky,
And why the moon is very white
As it rides the sky at night.

I have often wondered too
Why the bluebell is so blue,
And why the elm is straight and tall
And creepers climb my garden wall.

And tell me, Lord, why all things grow,
And why the wind and breezes blow,
And why a butterfly should fly
So crooked as it flutters by.

And tell me, Lord, why in the pool
The goldfish never are too cool,
And why the seasons come and go;
So many things I want to know.

Tell me, Lord, why the corn is gold,
Why oak trees are so big and old,
Why nightingales must sing at night
And glow-worms show a little light.

I want to know as well why cows
Lie still so long and browse and browse,
Why swift and swallow dart and turn –
Remember, Lord, I want to learn.

And you, dear Lord, such things must know
Because I think you made them so.

Clarence Winchester

The Land of Counterpane

When I was sick and lay a-bed
I had two pillows at my head,
And all my toys beside me lay
To keep me happy all the day.

And sometimes for an hour or so
I watched my leaden soldiers go,
With different uniforms and drills,
Among the bed-clothes through the hills;

And sometimes sent my ships in fleets
All up and down among the sheets;
Or brought my trees and houses out,
And planted cities all about.

I was the giant great and still
That sits upon the pillow-hill,
And sees before him, dale and plain,
The pleasant land of counterpane.

R. L. Stevenson

Hide and Seek

Hide and seek, says the Wind,
  In the shade of the woods;
Hide and seek, says the Moon,
  To the hazel buds;
Hide and seek, says the Cloud,
  Star on to star;
Hide and seek, says the Wave
  At the harbour bar;
Hide and seek, says I,
  To myself, and step
Out of the dream of Wake
  Into the dream of Sleep.

Walter de la Mare

Morning Prayer

Now another day is breaking,
Sleep was sweet and so is waking.
Dear Lord, I promised you last night
Never again to sulk or fight.
Such vows are easier to keep
When a child is sound asleep.
Today, O Lord, for your dear sake,
I'll try to keep them when awake.

Ogden Nash

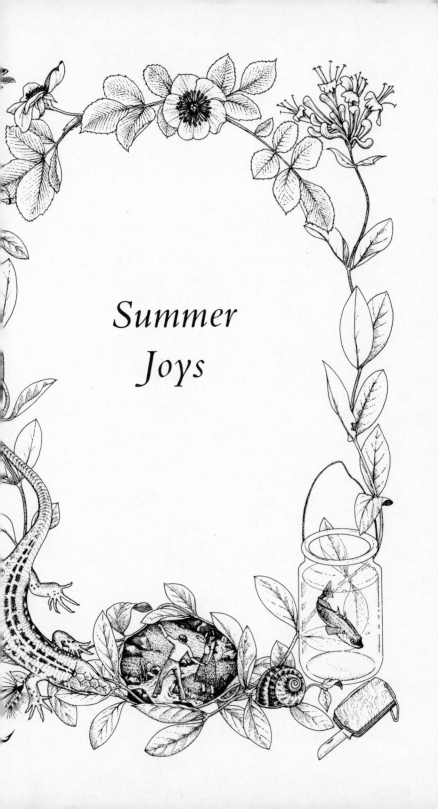

Summer
Joys

The pastures are clothed with flocks;
The valleys also are covered over with corn;
They shout for joy, they also sing.

The summer's flower is to the summer sweet wrote Shakes-peare, who also paid his beloved the beautiful compli-ment: *Shall I compare thee to a summer's day?*

We all love Summer, which so often comes with a burst of glory after a tempestuous Spring. Almost before we realise what is happening, once again the days are longer and the nights so often bright with stars, and whatever our age we think of it as the season of youth. It brings us days of sport in the sunshine, the excitement of travel, the anticipation of holidays with their long, lazy days. New places and new faces.

As the natural world moves on towards ripeness and fulfilment, so does the Christian year remind us, with its great Festivals, of God's purpose for us. Fittingly, after Easter Day in Spring, we are reminded that forty days later we celebrate the glorious Ascension, which is soon followed by the miracle and promise of Whitsun and the mysteries of Trinity Sunday.

I hope you will enjoy what I offer you for Summer. There is something for the youngest reader and I could not resist the passages about young love as described by Anne Frank. I believe you will agree that what this girl of fourteen wrote in her diary, to an imaginary friend, will live for all time. I have visited Amsterdam and been inside the house in which she hid with her family, while she was growing into a young woman. Not many Summer joys for Anne, who never left the family's hiding place until she, her parents and her friends, were taken away. Try to share her faith in God, her courage, her cheerfulness, her love of beauty – and indeed her faith in love itself.

For younger readers, there is Jane's midsummer birthday, which came from a book which I wrote nearly thirty years ago while I was living in a farmhouse with my young family. It is one of my favourites.

I believe *We Are Going to See the Rabbit*, on page 98, will start you wondering what is happening to our wonderful world; and I hope you will smile at the verses about the Green Woodpecker.

And perhaps when you have read through these extracts which to older readers may bring back some happy memories of happy summers, you will turn to page 90 and read again another favourite quotation from Shakespeare.

Summer days for me
When every leaf is on its tree;
When Robin's not a beggar,
And Jenny Wren's a bride,
And larks hang singing singing singing
Over the wheat fields wide —

Christina Rossetti

Answer to a Child's Question

Do you ask what the birds say?
  The sparrow, the dove,
The linnet and thrush say,
  'I love, and I love!'
In the winter they're silent,
  The wind is so strong;
What it says I don't know,
  But it sings a loud song.
But green leaves, and blossoms,
  And sunny warm weather,
And singing and loving –
  All come back together.
But the lark is so brimful
  Of gladness and love,
The green fields below him,
  The blue sky above,
That he sings, and he sings,
  And for ever sings he,
'I love my Love, and my Love loves me.'

Samuel Taylor Coleridge

Paper Boats

Day by day I float my paper boats one by one down the running stream. I hope that someone in some strange land will find them and know who I am.

I load my little boats with shiuli flowers from our garden and hope that these blooms of the dawn will be carried safely to land in the night . . .

. . . When night comes I bury my face in my arms and dream that my paper boats float on and on under the midnight stars.

Rabindranath Tagore

Where Go the Boats?

Dark brown is the river,
   Golden is the sand.
It flows along for ever,
   With trees on either hand.

Green leaves a–floating,
   Castles of the foam,
Boats of mine a–boating –
   Where will all come home?

On goes the river
   And out past the mill,
Away down the valley,
   Away down the hill.

Away down the river,
   A hundred miles or more,
Other little children
   Shall bring my boats ashore.

R. L. Stevenson

The May Magnificat

May is Mary's month, and I
Muse at that and wonder why:
  Her feasts follow reason,
  Dated due to season –

Candlemas, Lady Day;
But the Lady Month, May,
  Why fasten that upon her,
  With a feasting in her honour?

Is it only its being brighter
Than the most are must delight her?
  Is it opportunest
  And flowers finds soonest?

Ask of her, the mighty mother:
Her reply puts this other
  Question: What is Spring? –
  Growth in every thing –

Flesh and fleece, fur and feather,
Grass and greenworld all together;
  Star-eyed strawberry-breasted
  Throstle above her nested

Cluster of bugle blue eggs thin
Forms and warms the life within;
  And bird and blossom swell
  In sod or sheath or shell.

All things rising, all things sizing
Mary sees, sympathising
   With that world of good,
   Nature's motherhood.

Their magnifying of each its kind
With delight calls to mind
   How she did in her stored
   Magnify the Lord.

Well but there was more than this:
Spring's universal bliss
   Much, had much to say
   To offering Mary May.

When drop-of-blood-and-foam-dapple
Bloom lights the orchard-apple
   And thicket and thorp are merry
   With silver-surfèd cherry

And azuring-over greybell makes
Wood banks and brakes wash wet like lakes
   And magic cuckoo-call
   Caps, clears, and clinches all –

This ecstasy all through mothering earth
Tells Mary her mirth till Christ's birth
   To remember and exultation
   In God who was her salvation.

Gerard Manley Hopkins

Summer is Nigh!

Summer is nigh!
How do I know?

Why, this very day
A robin sat
On a tilting spray,
And merrily sang
A song of May.

Jack Frost has fled
From the rippling brook,
And a trout peeped out
From his shady nook.

A butterfly too
Flew lazily by,
And the willow catkins
Shook from on high
Their yellow dust
As I passed by:

And so I know
That summer is nigh.

Home Pictures in May

The sunshine bathes in clouds of many hues
And morning's feet are gemmed with early dews;
Warm daffodils about the garden beds
Peep through their pale slim leaves their golden heads,
Sweet earthly suns of spring; the gosling broods,
In coats of sunny green, about the road
Waddle in ecstasy; and in rich moods
The old hen leads her flickering chicks abroad,
Oft scuttling 'neath her wings to see the kite
Hang wavering o'er them in the Spring's blue light.
The sparrows round their new nests chirp with glee
And sweet the robin Spring's young luxury shares,
Tootling its song in feathery gooseberry tree
While watching worms the gardener's spade unbares.

John Clare

I Meant to Do my Work Today

I meant to do my work today –
But a brown bird sang in the apple tree,
And a butterfly flitted across the field,
And all the leaves were calling me.

And the wind went sighing over the land
Tossing the grasses to and fro,
And a rainbow held out its shining hand –
So what could I do but laugh and go?

Richard Le Gallienne

The Wind

I can get through a doorway without any key,
And strip the leaves from the great oak tree.

I can drive storm-clouds and shake tall towers,
Or steal through a garden and not wake the flowers.

Seas I can move and ships I can sink;
I can carry a house-top or the scent of a pink.

When I am angry I can rave and riot;
And when I am spent, I lie quiet as quiet.

James Reeves

'The Lucky Months'

Those born in the scented months of summer were the most favoured of all. To be able to boast that one's birthday was in June was as good as saying that one had had a silver mug for a christening present and the fairy godmother herself to give it.

My father was born in this gracious month and his large happy face was the epitome of summer weather to me. As his birthday was the last day of the month he only just managed to get into the time of roses and sunshine. There was never a quiet birthday feast for him for it was always haymaking time, when work went on from early dawn till the stars came out in the evening sky. I wore a pleated sun-bonnet and played among the haycocks, and rode in the hay-cart behind shire horses decked with honeysuckle and branches of the ash-tree. It was the season of strawberries and junkets. Thrice fortunate were those born in the month of June.

July and August also were lucky months, next to June in happiness. The garden was full of fruit, the house was wreathed in tea-roses. Clove carnations, sweet williams, delicate smells and pretty flowers abounded. I made dolls out of flaunting poppy-heads, and scent out of rose-petals. I slipped the gloves of the foxglove on my fingers, when I called 'Co-oop, Co-oop' to the cows and followed slowly after them across the dreaming fields. The meadows were cut, and they shone green as emerald like the lawns of a great house.

July's children were favoured and happy. Saint Swithin's Day came on the 15th, it is true, but even this day of anxiety about the weather was brightened for us because it was my mother's birthday. I went to the village with threepence, the fruit of many weeks of saving. I bought a china dog, or a dainty book of texts. My little brother, who had even less money, bought her a card. My father gave her nothing at all, but she was supremely happy, as we all sat down to the birthday tea with the best blue Wedgwood china on the table.

Alison Uttley
from Birthdays *in* Country Hoard

'Soon . . .'

Soon will the high Midsummer pomps come on,
   Soon will the musk carnations break and swell,
Soon shall we have gold-dusted snapdragon,
   Sweet-William with its homely cottage-smell,
     And stocks in fragrant blow;
Roses that down the alleys shine afar,
     And open, jasmine-muffled lattices,
     And groups under the dreaming garden-trees,
And the full moon, and the white evening-star.

Matthew Arnold
from Thyrsis

The First Pentecost

When the day of Pentecost had come, they were all together in one place. And suddenly a sound came from heaven like the rush of a mighty wind, and it filled all the house where they were sitting. And there appeared to them tongues as of fire, distributed and resting on each one of them. And they were all filled with the Holy Spirit and began to speak in other tongues, as the Spirit gave them utterance.

Acts, 2, 1–4

Pentecost, or Whitsun as this great festival is usually called in western Christendom, is not always celebrated with the importance which is its due. And yet the story of the first coming of the Holy Ghost is not only intensely dramatic, but also gloriously poetic. Ever since childhood, I have been impressed by this record of eleven men, plus a newcomer named Matthias chosen by lot to take the place of the traitor Judas, seated together in a nameless house 'when the day of Pentecost had come'. On the day of his ascension, their Lord had promised them, 'You shall receive power when the Holy Spirit has come upon you.'

I wanted to include in this anthology a quotation from the magnificent Old Testament, as well as my quotations from the glorious New, and so I add here the words of the Jewish prophet Joel, which the fisherman Peter quoted to the astonished crowd of 'devout men from every nation under heaven' who thronged the house to hear twelve simple Galileans speaking to them in their own languages. *M.S.*

Signs and Wonders

And in the last days it shall be, God declares,
That I will pour out my Spirit upon all flesh,
And your sons and your daughters shall prophesy,
And your young men shall see visions,
And your old men shall dream dreams;
Yea, and on my menservants and my maidservants
    in those days
I will pour out my Spirit; and they shall prophesy.
And I will show wonders in the heaven above
And signs on the earth beneath,
Blood, and fire, and vapour of smoke;
The sun shall be turned into darkness
And the moon into blood,
Before the day of the Lord comes,
The great and manifest day.
And it shall be that whoever calls on the name
    of the Lord
Shall be saved.

Joel, *2*, *28–32*
quoted by the Apostle Peter
Acts, *2*, *17–21*

Three Masts

Three masts has the thrusting ship,
Three masts will she wear
When she like Christ our Saviour
Walks on the watery stair.

One stands at the fore
   To meet the weather wild
As He who once in winter
   Was a little child.

One grows after
   From step to the sky
For Him who once was keel-hauled
   And hung up to die.

One stands amidships
   Between fore and mizzen
Pointing to Paradise
   For Him who is risen.

Three masts will grow on the green ship
   Before she quits the quay,
For Father, Son and Holy Ghost:
   Blessed Trinity.

Charles Causley

Green Woodpecker

When I were a-coming
Back home for my tea,
I hears an old Yaffle
Up top of a tree.
And standing beneath him,
I tries to make out
What that there old Yaffle
Were laughing about.

His cap it were scarlet,
His jacket were green –
The finest old Yaffle
That ever were seen.
He laughed and he laughed
As he sat on his bough.
But I couldn't make sense
Of that Yaffle, nohow.

'You silly old Yaffle,'
I started to bawl,
'A-sitting there, laughing
At nothing at all!'
And Yaffle, he answered –
I swear this be true:
'You silly old juggins,
I'm laughing at you!'

Reginald Arkell

Cherry Tree

The Chaffinch flies fast
  To the red cherry tree,
And sings as he goes:
  'All for me! All for me!'

The Speckled Brown Thrush
  Upon fluttering wing
Goes flying and scolds:
  'Greedy thing! Greedy thing!'

The chattering Starling,
  He visits there, too,
And cries as he flies:
  'Leave a few! Leave a few!'

But the Blackbird retreats
  As the others advance,
And calls to them, laughing:
  'Not a chance! Not a chance!'

                    Ivy Eastwick

Sunning

Old Dog lay in the summer sun
Much too lazy to rise and run.
He flapped an ear
At a buzzing fly;
He winked a half-opened
Sleepy eye;
He scratched himself
On an itching spot;
As he dozed on the porch
When the sun was hot.
He whimpered a bit
From force of habit,
While he lazily dreamed
Of chasing a rabbit.
But Old Dog happily lay in the sun,
Much too lazy to rise and run.

James S. Tippett

Haytime

It's Midsummer Day
And they're cutting the hay
Down in the meadow just over the way,
The children all run
For a frolic, and fun –
For haytime is playtime out in the sun.

It's Midsummer Day,
And they're raking the hay
Down in the meadow all golden and gay,
They're tossing it high
Beneath the June sky,
And the hay rakes are spreading it out to dry.

Irene F. Pawsey

'A Midsummer Birthday'

Every morning now the sun rose high into a clear blue sky and by the time Jane rode up the hill to the beech trees it was already hot. Her uncle's cornfields blazed with scarlet poppies and a handsome lime tree in the rectory garden sang with the music of myriads of bees seeking the honey of the little flowers. In the lane where the tall wild parsley towered above the nettles in the ditch, the butterflies danced in the sunshine and all day long over the common and above the fields the larks sang and sang. Jane never tired of watching the larks soaring into the blue sky but neither Richard nor she ever found a nest although they often searched.

The fine weather held and Midsummer Day dawned with a mist in the hollows that heralded heat. When they reached the field the horse-drawn mowing-machine was already clacking its way round. The edges had been cut and the grass was falling in flat swathes at one side. Uncle William leaned on the gate and for a long minute said nothing. Jane, happy and excited, looked up at his brown wrinkled face and then followed his glance to the wide expanse of flower-decked hay waiting for the reaper. As she watched, the surface rippled in the warm wind that came in puffs from the south. Tall white marguerites, golden buttercups, pink and white campion and spears of red sorrel swayed gently in the breeze.

'Happy birthday, Janey!' Richard said as he came to meet her.

By noon it was too hot to stay in the sun so they moved into the shade of two big elms by the gate. George unharnessed the horses and gave them their nosebags, and clumped off down the lane to his cottage.

Sidney stopped the tractor and sat down under the hedge and lit a cigarette. Uncle William stayed with the children and shared their lunch and then lay back and went to sleep for twenty minutes. Jane felt sleepy too and even Richard was quiet as he leaned against the trunk of the tree and looked up through the leaves to the sky.

In the afternoon they worked by turning the wind-rows with long wooden rakes. The air was sweet with the smell of the hay and the sun was so hot that Richard took off his shirt.

They were spreading the cloth for tea under the elms when there came several loud 'Coo-ees' and calls of 'Janey! *Janey!*'

Five girls and two boys were standing on the bottom rung of the gate and they all waved furiously when Jane stood up.

'Happy birthday, Janey!'

Malcolm Saville
from Jane's Country Year

'I Know a Bank'

I know a bank where the wild thyme blows,
Where oxlips and the nodding violet grows;
Quite over-canopied with luscious woodbine,
With sweet musk roses, and with eglantine:
There sleeps Titania sometime of the night,
Lull'd in these flowers with dances and delight;
And there the snake throws her enamell'd skin,
Weed wide enough to wrap a fairy in . . .

William Shakespeare
from A Midsummer Night's Dream

'This is London'

This is the first time I have ever truly
seen that London whose sweet Thames runs
softly; that minstrel mermaid of a town,
the water-streeted eight-million-headed
village in a blaze. This is London . . .
The arches of the bridges leap into light;
the moon clocks glow; the river sings;
the harmonious pavilions are happy.
And this is what London should always
be like, till St Paul's falls down and the
sea slides over the strand.

Dylan Thomas
Written at the time of
the Festival of Britain, 1952

'The Rain . . . The Sun'

There was a roaring in the wind all night;
The rain came heavily and fell in floods;
But now the sun is rising calm and bright;
The birds are singing in the distant woods;
Over his own sweet voice the Stock-dove broods;
The Jay makes answer as the Magpie chatters;
And all the air is filled with pleasant noise of waters.

All things that love the sun are out of doors;
The sky rejoices in the morning's birth;
The grass is bright with rain drops; – on the moors
The hare is running races in her mirth;
And with her feet she from the plashy earth
Raises a mist; that, glittering in the sun,
Runs with her all the way, wherever she doth run.

William Wordsworth
from The Leech-Gatherer

A Rainy Day

With weights of tears the bluebell broke,
The tall white campion wept in sleeping,
And all the humming honey-folk
A fast were keeping.

Mary Webb

Boy Fishing

I am cold and alone,
On my tree-root sitting as still as stone.
The fish come to my net. I scorned the sun,
The voices on the road, and they have gone.
My eyes are buried in the cold pond, under
The cold, spread leaves; my thoughts are silver-wet.
I have ten stickleback, a half-day's plunder,
Safe in my jar. I shall have ten more yet.

E. J. Scovell

The Little Green Orchard

Some one is always sitting there,
     In the little green orchard;
  Even when the sun is high,
  In noon's unclouded sky,
  And faintly droning goes
  The bee from rose to rose,
Some one in shadow is sitting there,
     In the little green orchard.

Yes, and when twilight's falling softly
     On the little green orchard;
  When the grey dew distils
  And every flower-cup fills;
  When the last blackbird says,
  'What – what!' and goes her way – ssh!
I have heard voices calling softly
     In the little green orchard.

Not that I am afraid of being there,
     In the little green orchard;
  Why, when the moon's been bright,
  Shedding her lonesome light,
  And moths like ghosties come,
  And the horned snail leaves home:
I've sat there, whispering and listening there,
     In the little green orchard;

Only it's strange to be feeling there,
   In the little green orchard,
 Whether you paint or draw,
 Dig, hammer, chop, or saw;
 When you are most alone,
 All but the silence gone . . .
Some one is waiting and watching there,
   In the little green orchard.

       Walter de la Mare

Summer Evening

The sandy cat by the Farmer's chair
Mews at his knee for dainty fare;
Old Rover in his moss-greened house
Mumbles a bone, and barks at a mouse.
In the dewy fields the cattle lie
Chewing the cud 'neath a fading sky;
Dobbin at manger pulls his hay:
Gone is another summer's day.

Walter de la Mare

Under the Moon

After a while I came to a great gnarled hawthorn hedge
. . . Within its precincts dwelt intense sweetness; and
there I stayed, looking into the next field through an
interstice of the twisty branches. The young rabbits
were out under the moon, wild with excitement, the
very soul of gaiety: they were washing their faces, dashing off at a tangent, leaping over lakes of pale light.
Parents, grandparents, and great-grandparents were
there, frisking with abandon in the athletic manner of
Dickens's old folk at Christmas. Off went a stripling,
bounding over a lake, landing in the middle, dashing
away with a delighted kick, as if he said – 'Ha! Only
moonshine water!' A grandfather, watching as he
trimmed his whiskers, was fired to do likewise, glee-
fully beating the record. What is that stir in the grass at
the root of the thorn? A grave hedgehog slips out and
watches in a superior manner. Suddenly she becomes

nfected with the revelry, and rushes away at a surpris-
ng pace to share the general energy of enjoyment.
Behind her come four minute hedgehogs, replicas of
heir mother, except that their spines are nearly white
nd their ears hang down. Like her, they run in the
nanner of toy animals upon invisible wheels. They all
;o at a speed one could not have believed possible,
oining in the fun, recklessly negotiating the fairy rings;
nd their absurd little shadows follow madly after.

Mary Webb
from The Spring of Joy

We are Going to See the Rabbit

We are going to see the rabbit,
We are going to see the rabbit.
Which rabbit? people say
Which rabbit? ask the children
Which rabbit?
The only rabbit,
The only rabbit in England,
Sitting behind a barbed-wire fence
Under the floodlights, neon lights,
Sodium lights,
Nibbling grass
On the only patch of grass
In England, in England
(Except the grass by the hoardings
Which doesn't count.)
We are going to see the rabbit
And we must be there on time.

First we shall go by escalator,
And then we shall go by underground,
And then we shall go by motorway
And then by helicopterway,
And the last ten yards we shall have to go
On foot.

And now we are going
All the way to see the rabbit,
We are nearly there,
We are longing to see it,
And so is the crowd
Which is here in thousands.

With mounted policemen
And big loudspeakers
And bands and banners,
And everyone has come a long way.
But soon we shall see it
Sitting and nibbling
The blades of grass
On the only patch of grass
In – but something has gone wrong!
Why is everyone so angry,
Why is everyone jostling
And slanging and complaining?

The rabbit has gone
Yes, the rabbit has gone.
He has actually burrowed down into the earth
And made himself a warren, under the earth,
Despite all these people.
And what shall we do?
What can we do?

It is all a pity, you must be disappointed,
Go home and do something else for today,
Go home again, go home for today.
For you cannot hear the rabbit, under the earth,
Remarking rather sadly to himself, by himself,
As he rests in his warren, under the earth:
'It won't be long, they are bound to come,
They are bound to come and find me, even here.'

Alan Brownjohn

'Good and Dear and Beautiful'

*In May, 1940, early in the Second World War, Holland was
occupied by the German Army. In the months and years that
followed, many Jews were sent to the concentration camps set
up by the Nazi regime, and there were killed. The Frank
family, being Jewish, were in great danger, and in 1942 they
went into hiding in a set of sealed-up rooms at the back of an
office building in Amsterdam. Sharing the hiding-place with
Mr and Mrs Frank and their two teenage daughters, Margot
and Anne, were four other Jews: Mr and Mrs Van Daan, their
son Peter, and a dentist, Dr Dussel. Anne Frank was thirteen
when first they went into hiding. In her diary she talked to an
imaginary friend, Kitty.*

Wednesday, February 23, 1944

Dear Kitty,

It's lovely weather outside and I've quite perked up
since yesterday. Nearly every morning I go to the attic
where Peter works to blow the stuffy air out of my
lungs. From my favourite spot on the floor I look up at
the blue sky and the bare chestnut tree, on whose
branches little raindrops glisten like silver, and at the
seagulls and other birds as they glide on the wind.

He stood with his head against a thick beam, and I sat
down. We breathed the fresh air, looked outside and
both felt that the spell should not be broken by words.
We remained like this for a long time, and when he had
to go up to the loft to chop wood, I knew that he was a
nice fellow. He climbed the ladder, and I followed; then
he chopped wood for about a quarter of an hour, during
which time we still remained silent. I watched him from
where I stood, he was obviously doing his best to show
off his strength. But I looked out of the open window

too, over a large area of Amsterdam, over all the roofs and on to the horizon, which was such a pale blue that it was hard to see the dividing line. 'As long as this exists,' I thought, 'and I may live to see it, this sunshine, the cloudless skies, while this lasts, I cannot be unhappy.'

The best remedy for those who are afraid, lonely or unhappy, is to go outside, somewhere where they can be quite alone with the heavens, nature and God. Because only then does one feel that all is as it should be and that God wishes to see people happy, amidst the simple beauty of nature. As long as this exists, and it certainly always will, I know that then there will always be comfort for every sorrow, whatever the circumstances may be. And I firmly believe that nature brings solace in all troubles.

Oh, who knows, perhaps it won't be long before I can share this overwhelming feeling of bliss with someone who feels the way I do about it.

Yours, Anne.

Anne believed that Peter loved her, but he said and did nothing to show it. Confined as they were, she did not like to run after him by going upstairs; yet there was nowhere else she could go, and talking to him was a great comfort to her, after the daily squabbles, scoldings and fears that filled their lives in the cramped hiding-place. On the evening of April 15th, something happened that gave Anne great happiness:

Sunday morning, just before eleven o'clock,
16th April, 1944

Darlingest Kitty,
Remember yesterday's date, for it is a very important day in my life. Surely it is a great day for every girl when

she receives her first kiss? Well, then, it is just as important for me too! Bram's kiss on my right cheek doesn't count any more, likewise the one from Mr Walker on my right hand.

How did I suddenly come by this kiss? Well, I will tell you.

Yesterday evening at eight o'clock I was sitting with Peter on his divan. It wasn't long before his arm went round me. 'Let's move up a bit,' I said, 'then I don't bump my head against the cupboard.' He moved up, almost into the corner, I laid my arm under his and across his back, and he just about buried me, because his arm was hanging on my shoulder.

Now we've sat like this on other occasions, but never so close together as yesterday. He held me firmly against him, my left shoulder against his chest; already my heart began to beat faster, but we had not finished yet. He didn't rest until my head was on his shoulder and his against it. When I sat upright again after about five minutes, he soon took my head in his hands and laid it against him once more. Oh, it was so lovely, I couldn't talk much, the joy was too great. He stroked my cheek and arm a bit awkwardly, played with my curls and our heads lay touching most of the time. I can't tell you, Kitty, the feeling that ran through me all the while. I was too happy for words, and I believe he was as well.

We got up at half-past eight. Peter put on his gym shoes, so that when we toured the house he couldn't make a noise, and I stood beside him. How it came so suddenly, I don't know, but before we went downstairs he kissed me, through my hair, half on my left cheek, half on my ear; I tore downstairs without looking round, and am simply longing for today!

Yours, Anne.

A few weeks before Peter's kiss, when Anne was hoping all day long to be close to him, and he was still shy and silent, she wrote a long entry in her diary. In this she compared herself with the lively, flirtatious, forward and chattering child she had been in early 1942. She recalled the painful adjustment to life in hiding: first quarrels, bickering, her own quick impertinent answers; then fits of tears and wishing that she could recapture her old loving dependence on her father; at last self-reliance and a new inner quiet.

Tuesday, 7th March, 1944

. . . in the evening, when I lie in bed and end my prayers with the words 'I thank you, God, for all that is good and dear and beautiful,' I am filled with joy. Then I think about the 'good' of going into hiding, of my health and with my whole being of the 'dearness' of Peter, of that which is still embryonic and impressionable and which we neither of us dare to name or touch, of that which will come some time; love, the future, happiness and of the 'beauty' which exists in the world; the world, nature, beauty and all, all that is exquisite and fine.

I don't think then of all the misery, but of the beauty that still remains. This is one of the things that Mummy and I are so entirely different about. Her counsel when one feels melancholy is: 'Think of all the misery in the world and be thankful that you are not sharing it!' My advice is: 'Go outside, to the fields, enjoy nature and the sunshine, go out and try to recapture happiness in yourself and in God. Think of all the beauty that's still left in and around you and be happy!'

I don't see how Mummy's idea can be right, because then how are you supposed to behave if you are going through the misery yourself? Then you are lost. On the contrary, I've found that there is always some beauty left – in nature, sunshine, freedom, in yourself; these can

all help you. Look at these things, then you find yoursel
again, and God, and then you regain your balance.

And whoever is happy, will make others happy too
He who has courage and faith will never perish in mis
ery!

Yours, Anne

The radiant happiness of April 16 gave way to new anxietie
as the summer drew on; but the resolution of March 7 remaine
— we must hope it never failed her.

'*I know what I want,*' *Anne wrote,* '*I have a goal, an*
opinion, I have a religion and love. Let me be myself and the
I am satisfied. If God lets me live,' *she said,* '*I shall not remai*
insignificant, I shall work in the world and for mankind. An
now I know that first and foremost I shall require courage an
cheerfulness.'

On August 4, 1944, when Anne and the others had been i
hiding for two years, they were betrayed to the Nazis. Arme
German police and Dutch Nazis raided the hiding-place an
sent the prisoners to Westerbork, the camp about which Ann
had had nightmares. Then they were sent on to the terribl
concentration camp at Auschwitz in Poland. Peter's fathe
was killed there, and there too, on January 5 1945, Anne'
mother died. Anne and her sister Margot had been separate
from the others a few weeks earlier, in the winter of 1944, an
sent to another camp, Belsen. Here in February 1945 Margo
died of typhus. Of all those who had hidden in 'the hous
behind', only Anne's father came back alive to Amsterdam
when peace was at last declared: Peter Van Daan disappeared
with thousands of other prisoners, when Auschwitz wa
evacuated by the Germans: and a few days after Margot'
death, Anne herself died, in March 1945, two months befor
the war ended. She was fifteen.

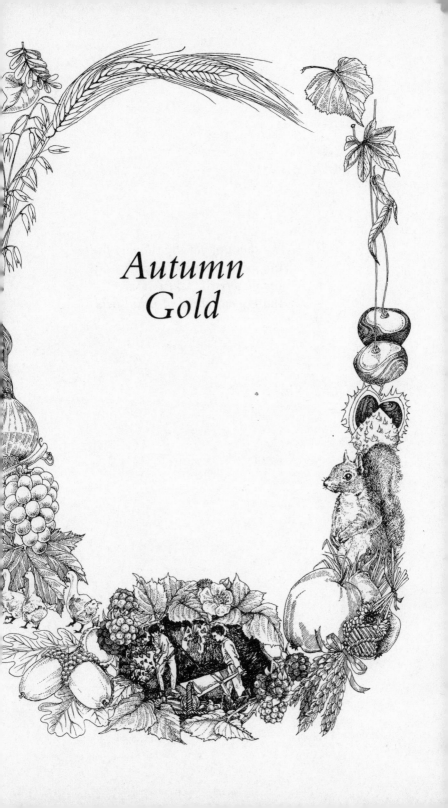

Autumn
Gold

The shouting for thy summer fruits
And for thy harvest is fallen,
And gladness is taken away,
And joy out of the plentiful field.

Autumn does not seem to come as suddenly as Spring
follows Winter. Birth is quicker than maturity and so, in
this section, I have tried to show that the year sinks
peacefully into the sleep of Winter. I hope you will
realise how sensitive are many of the poets whose work
I have selected to the wonders of Nature. True that
sometimes the leaves come tumbling in a single night,
but although the days grow shorter, many of us pick
roses in October, to remind us of Summer days.

So because Autumn is a time for remembering, I have
tried to find some passages which have meant much to
me as I have journeyed through the seasons. Such
memories are particularly precious because my own
Golden Wedding is the most recent and important of
them all. And many, many years before that, I
remember when as a very young man, how I was
influenced by *These I Have Loved* by a poet killed in the
1914–18 war in the first flush of his youth.

Because I have daughters and granddaughters as well
as sons and grandsons I commend the words with
which Laurie Lee, the author of *Cider with Rosie*, greeted
the birth of his first daughter.

In the Christian's calendar we remember first the
mighty St Michael and his angels, then the majesty of
All Saints, sometimes called All Hallows, and the
mysteries of All Souls.

I saw old Autumn in the misty morn
Stand shadowless like Silence, listening
To silence . . .

Thomas Hood

Something Told the Wild Geese

Something told the wild geese
   It was time to go.
Though the fields lay golden
   Something whispered, 'Snow.'
Leaves were green and stirring,
   Berries, lustre-glossed,
But beneath warm feathers
   Something cautioned, 'Frost.'
All the sagging orchards
   Steamed with amber spice,
But each wild breast stiffened
   At remembered ice.
Something told the wild geese
   It was time to fly –
Summer sun was on their wings,
   Winter in their cry.

Rachel Field

If I Should Ever by Chance

If I should ever by chance grow rich
I'll buy Codham, Cockridden and Childerditch,
Roses, Pyrgo and Lapwater,
And let them all to my elder daughter.
The rent I shall ask of her will be only
Each year's first violets, white and lonely,
The first primroses and orchises –
She must find them before I do, that is.
But if she finds a blossom on furze
Without rent they shall all for ever be hers,
Whenever I am sufficiently rich:
Codham, Cockridden and Childerditch,
Roses, Pyrgo and Lapwater –
I shall give them all to my elder daughter.

Edward Thomas

Second Chance

I have got a daughter, whose life is already separate from
mine, whose will already follows its own directions,
and who has quickly corrected my woolly preconcep-
tions of her by being something remorselessly different.
She is the child of herself and will be what she is. I am
merely the keeper of her temporary helplessness.

Even so, with luck, she can alter me; indeed, is doing
so now. At this stage in my life she will give me more

than she gets, and may even later become my keeper.

But if I could teach her anything at all – by unloading upon her some of the ill-tied parcels of my years – I'd like it to be acceptance and a holy relish for life. To accept with gladness the fact of being a woman – when she'll find all nature to be on her side. If pretty, to thank God and enjoy her luck and not start beefing about being loved for her mind. To be willing to give pleasure without feeling loss of face, to prefer charm to the vanity of aggression, and not to deliver her powers and mysteries into the opposite camp by wishing to compete with men.

In this way, I believe – though some of her sisters may disapprove – she might know some happiness and also spread some around. And as a brief tenant of this precious and irreplaceable world, I'd ask her to preserve life both in herself and others. . . .

For the rest, may she be my own salvation, for any man's child is his second chance. In this role I see her leading me back to my beginnings, re-opening rooms I'd locked and forgotten, stirring the dust in my mind by re-asking the big questions – as any child can do.

But in my case, perhaps, just not too late; she persuades me there may yet be time, that with her, my tardy but bright-eyed pathfinder, I may return to that wood which long ago I fled from, but which together we may now enter and know.

Laurie Lee
from The Firstborn

Cock-Crow

Out of the wood of thoughts that grows by night
To be cut down by the sharp axe of light, –
Out of the night, two cocks together crow,
Cleaving the darkness with a silver blow:
And bright before my eyes twin trumpeters stand,
Heralds of splendour, one at either hand,
Each facing each as in a coat of arms:
The milkers lace their boots up at the farms.

Edward Thomas

'A Son and Heir'

September was the last chance for a lucky child. To be
born in this month, one just arrived on earth in time to
escape the stormy blasts of the back end of the year. It
was the season of brown cob-nuts and sweet Spanish
chestnuts, of yellow apples and freckled pears. In that
month the tallest ladders were carried from the stack-
yard and reared against the orchard trees. Clothes-
baskets were brought in the thick grass ready to be
heaped with the loads of Pippins and Quarrendens and
Keswicks. We stood on the walls and shook the damson
trees and hit the spreading boughs. Then we hunted in
the nettle-beds underneath to find the purple fruit.
Damsons grew half-wild in many unexpected places,
little old trees in pig-cote garde, in croft and hedgerow,

overhanging the water trough and the walls. September was the month of plenty when the granaries were filled in preparation for winter. It would be splendid to enter life with the certainty of a Harvest Festival and a Flower Show and apple-picking in one's birthday month, I thought. . . .

My brother came into the world to be the son and heir in September. My father was up in the filbert-trees gathering the nuts. That was indeed a romantic entry into the world! My father was hidden in the tall bushy trees which grew on the steep slope of the field. He had a couple of baskets and they were piled with the clusters of frilly-coated 'filberds'. His ears must have been pricked for the news, for the doctor was in the house. Suddenly the back door opened, and our old nurse appeared. She excitedly called down the field to the trees shaking and trembling under his weight.

'Master! Master! A son! You've gotten a son at last,' she shouted, and she blew a whistle and rang a bell to summons him.

Didn't he clamber down double-quick and hurry up the steep hillside across the meadow to the bedroom where my mother lay! He was twice as quick as he had been when I was born, he said, for here was a boy, a son and heir, the first boy born at the farm for fifty years. I felt envious of that intimate connection with 'filberds', and when they said my brother's eyes were hazel, I was sure the colour was due to the nut-picking at the baby's birth.

Alison Uttley
from Birthdays *in* Country Hoard

Autumn in the City

Sometimes in September I half expect to turn out of the Strand into a lane heavy with fruit, the ghost of some ancient autumn. Autumn is eternal, and perhaps she whispers in the stone forests of London as she whispered in the streets of Babylon, 'Wait only a little and you shall bear fruit again.'

H. V. Morton
from The London Year

Down through the ancient Strand
The spirit of October, mild and boon
And sauntering, takes his way
This golden end of afternoon,
As though the corn stood yellow in all the land,
And the ripe apples dropped in the harvest moon.

W. E. Henley
from A London Voluntary

'Harvest Festival'

Blood-dark dahlias, bronze corn-coloured chrysan-
themums, mauve Michaelmas daisies – these are the
flowers that wrangle with the loud saints above them in
hot-coloured jubilation. Bunches of grapes hang from
the pulpit over bowing sheaves, or from the lectern
where wheat and barley are crossed under the golden
bird. Around the font, and along the window ledges,
and each side of the chancel steps, there are pools and
tumuli of apples, melons, plums and peaches; potatoes,
turnips and cucumbers; baskets of figs, currants, rasp-
berries and nuts; great dropsical marrows; and loaves of
bread confessing to sheaves.

Laurence Whistler

The Golden Boy

In March he was buried
    And nobody cried
Buried in the dirt
    Nobody protested
Where grubs and insects
    That nobody knows
With outer-space faces
    That nobody loves
Can make him their feast
    As if nobody cared.

But the Lord's mother
    Full of her love
Found him underground
    And wrapped him with love
As if he were her baby
    Her own born love
She nursed him with miracles
    And starry love
And he began to live
    And to thrive on her love

He grew night and day
    And his murderers were glad
He grew like a fire
    And his murderers were happy
He grew lithe and tall
    And his murderers were joyful
He toiled in the fields
    And his murderers cared for him
He grew a gold beard
    And his murderers laughed.

With terrible steel
  They slew him in the furrow
With terrible steel
  They beat his bones from him
With terrible steel
  They ground him to powder
They baked him in ovens
  They sliced him on tables
They ate him they ate him
  They ate him they ate him

Thanking the Lord
Thanking the Wheat
Thanking the Bread
For bringing them Life
Today and Tomorrow
Out of the dirt.

Ted Hughes

Promise

Autumn has come again; the falling leaves
Are shed as old men's years, and drift away.
Evening more swiftly steals across the day,
And love in pain for the dead summer grieves.
How quiet are all the old deserted eaves.
The sky is pale – and the hills are grey
With mist, save where a solitary ray
Of golden light a fading flower deceives.
The lanes are russet with the touch of time
And lamps are earlier lit for husbandmen
Who homing sing in melancholy rhyme
Their ancient songs of crag and hill and fen.
And while the days inspire no song sublime
The tired earth sleeps only to wake again!

Clarence Winchester

Michaelmas : September 29
The Feast of St Michael and All Angels

'All the Angels'

She had painted all the angels she had ever heard about;
the four archangels, Michael, Gabriel, Raphael and
Asrael, superb creatures with huge wings like the feathered golden clouds she could see out of the window
when the sun was setting; the warrior angels with their
swords in their hands and flame in their eyes; seraphs
with their six wings, purple and blue wings like the
shadows that crept across the Market Place when the
first stars shone out and the earth veiled her face in awe
of them, covering their eyes before the eyes of God; the
guardian angels, less well dressed than the others, a little
overworked and harassed because their human charges
gave them such a lot of trouble, but very lovely all the
same; and jolly fat little bodiless cherubs like the carv-
ings in her room.

Elizabeth Goudge
from Sister of the Angels

Matthew, Mark, Luke and John,
Bless the bed that I lie on,
Four corners to my bed,
Four angels round my head,
One to watch, one to pray,
And two to bear my soul away.

The Choirmaster's Burial

He often would ask us
That, when he died,
After playing so many
To their last rest,
If out of us any
Should here abide,
And it would not task us,
We would with our lutes
Play over him
By his grave-brim
The psalm he liked best –
The one whose sense suits
'Mount Ephraim' –
And perhaps we should seem
To him, in Death's dream,
Like the seraphim.

As soon as I knew
That his spirit was gone
I thought this his due,
And spoke thereupon –

'I think,' said the vicar,
'A read service quicker
Than viols out of doors
In these frosts and hoars.
That old-fashioned way
Requires a fine day,
And it seems to me
It had better not be.'

Hence, that afternoon,
Though never knew he
That his wish could not be,
To get through it faster
They buried the master
Without any tune.

But 'twas said that, when
At the dead of next night
The vicar looked out,
There struck on his ken
Throngèd roundabout,
Where the frost was graying
The headstoned grass,
A band all in white
Like the saints in church-glass,
Singing and playing
The ancient stave
By the choirmaster's grave.

Such the tenor man told
When he had grown old.

Thomas Hardy •

October

I've brought you nuts and hops;
And when the leaf drops, why, the walnut drops.
Crack your first nut and light your first fire,
Roast your first chestnut crisp on the bar;
Make the logs sparkle, stir the blaze higher,
Logs are as cheery as sun or as star,
Logs we can find wherever we are.
Spring one soft day will open the leaves,
Spring one bright day will lure back the flowers;
Never fancy my whistling wind grieves,
Never fancy I've tears in my showers;
Dance, night and days! and dance on, my hours!

Christina Rossetti

'With this Ring'

'Thee, Mary, with this ring I wed,'
So, fourteen years ago, I said.
Behold another ring! 'For what?'
To wed thee o'er again – why not?

With that first ring I married youth,
Grace, beauty, innocence, and truth;
Taste long admir'd, sense long rever'd,
And all my Molly then appear'd.

If she, by merit since disclos'd,
Prove twice the woman I suppos'd,
I plead that double merit now,
To justify a double vow.

Here, then, today – with faith as sure,
With ardour as intense and pure,
As when amidst the rites divine
I took thy troth and plighted mine, –
To thee, sweet girl, my second ring,
A token and a pledge, I bring;
With this I wed, till death us part,
Thy riper virtues to my heart;
Those virtues which, before untried,
The wife has added to the bride –

For why? – They show me every hour
Honour's high thought, affection's power,
Discretion's deed, sound judgement's sentence,
And teach me all things – but repentance.

Samuel Bishop
'To his wife
on the fourteenth anniversary
of her Wedding-Day, with a Ring.'

St Francis's Day : October 4

A Robin Redbreast in a Cage
Puts all Heaven in a Rage . . .

A Skylark wounded in the wing –
A Cherubim does cease to sing . . .

He who shall hurt the little Wren
Shall never be belov'd by Men

William Blake

St Francis and the Birds

When Francis preached love to the birds
They listened, fluttered, throttled up
Into the blue like a flock of words

Released for fun from his holy lips.
Then wheeled back, whirred about his head,
Pirouetted on brothers' capes,

Danced on the wing, for sheer joy played
And sang, like images took flight.
Which was the best poem Francis made,

His argument true, his tone light.

Seamus Heaney

Desiderata

Go placidly amid the clamour of life, and remember the peace to be found in silence. Speak your truth quietly, listen to others but avoid loud and aggressive people who vex the spirit. Do not compare yourself with others – there will always be greater and lesser persons and you may become vain or bitter. Enjoy your achievements as well as your plans. Keep interest in your own life plan. It is a real possession. Be cautious in your affairs for the world is full of trickery, but do not let this blind you to virtue in others – many strive for high ideals and life is full of heroism. Be yourself – do not feign affection and do not be cynical about love, for in the face of all avidity and disenchantment love is perennial as the grass. Grow older gracefully surrendering the things of youth when the time comes. Nurture strength of spirit to shield you in misfortune. Do not allow yourself to become distressed by imaginings. Many fears come out of fatigue and loneliness. Have self discipline but be gentle with yourself. You are a child of the Universe, no less than the trees and the stars. You have a right to be here. And whether or not it is clear to you no doubt the Universe is unfolding as it should. Therefore be at peace with God, whatever you conceive him to be and whatever your labour and aspirations. Keep peace with your soul and be true to it. With all life's sham, drudgery and broken dreams it is still a *beautiful* world. Go carefully. Strive to be happy.

'These I Have Loved'

. . These I have loved:
White plates and cups, clean-gleaming,
Ringed with blue lines; and feathery, faery dust;
Wet roofs, beneath the lamp-light; the strong crust
Of friendly bread; and many-tasting food;
Rainbows; and the blue bitter smoke of wood;
And radiant raindrops couching in cool flowers;
And flowers themselves, that sway through sunny hours,
Dreaming of moths that drink them under the moon;
Then, the cool kindliness of sheets, that soon
Smooth away trouble; and the rough male kiss
Of blankets; grainy wood; live hair that is
Shining and free; blue-massing clouds; the keen
Unpassioned beauty of a great machine;
The benison of hot water; furs to touch;
The good smell of old clothes; and other such—
The comfortable smell of friendly fingers,
Hair's fragrance, and the musty reek that lingers
About dead leaves and last year's ferns . . .

Rupert Brooke
from The Great Lover

'Oh, Shall I Never'

Oh, shall I never, never be home again?
Meadows of England shining in the rain
Spread wide your daisied lawns: your ramparts green
With briar fortify, with blossom screen
Till my far morning – and O streams that slow
And pure and deep through plains and playlands go,
For me your love and all your kingcups store,
And – dark militia of the southern shore,
Old fragrant friends – preserve me the last lines
Of that long saga which you sang me, pines,
When, lonely boy, beneath the chosen tree
I listened, with my eyes upon the sea. . . . .

James Elroy Flecker
from Brumana

Four Ducks on a Pond

Four ducks on a pond,
A grass bank beyond,
A blue sky of spring,
White clouds on the wing;
What a little thing
To remember for years –
To remember with tears.

William Allingham

Dirge in Woods

A wind sways the pines,
  And below
Not a breath of wild air;
Still as the mosses that glow
On the flooring and over the lines
Of the roots here and there.
The pine-tree drops its dead;
They are quiet, as under the sea.
Overhead, overhead
Rushes life in a race,
As the clouds the clouds chase;
  And we go,
And we drop like the fruits of the tree,
  Even we,
  Even so.

George Meredith

Hallowe'en : October 31

'A Day to Remember'

The 31st of October, All Hallows' Eve, was an auspici ous date, a festival half-magical, half-religious. We cracked nuts before the fire, and threw apple peel ove the left shoulder, to find the initial of the one we shoul marry. We bobbed for apples in a pancheon of water or the kitchen table, and wet the tips of our noses as w stooped over the bowl. We had prayers in the kitchen a night, and we thought of the souls of the departed. Tha was the date for the birthday of one who would hav powers over the unseen, one who could hear the talk o the trees as they tossed and cried on winter nights, on who could see the wind and know the stars. All Hal lows' Eve was a day to remember, as the autumn slippe out of its cloak of leaves and naked winter came to tak its place.

Alison Uttle
from Birthdays *in* Country Hoar

For All the Saints

For all the saints who from their labours rest,
Who thee by faith before the world confessed,
Thy name, O Jesus, be for ever blest: *Alleluya!*

Thou wast their rock, their fortress and their might;
Thou, Lord, their captain in the well-fought fight;
Thou in the darkness drear their one true light:
                         Alleluya!

O may thy soldiers, faithful, true and bold,
Fight as the saints who nobly fought of old,
And win, with them, the victor's crown of gold:
                         Alleluya!

The golden evening brightens in the west;
Soon, soon to faithful warriors cometh rest;
Sweet is the calm of paradise the blest: *Alleluya!*

But lo! there breaks a yet more glorious day;
The saints triumphant rise in bright array:
The King of Glory passes on his way: *Alleluya!*

From earth's wide bounds, from ocean's farthest coast,
Through gates of pearl streams in the countless host,
Singing to Father, Son, and Holy Ghost:
                   Alleluya. Alleluya!

Bishop W. W. How

On All Souls' Day

Last night they lit your glass with wine
And brought for you the sweet soul-cake,
And blessed the room with candle-shine
For the grave journey you would make.

They told me not to stir between
The midnight strokes of one and two,
And I should see you come again
To view the scene that once you knew.

'Good night,' they said, and journeyed on.
I turned the key, and – turning – smiled,
And in the quiet house alone
I slept serenely as a child.

Innocent was that sleep, and free,
And when the first of morning shone
I had no need to gaze and see
If crumb, or bead of wine, had gone.

My heart was easy as this bloom
Of waters rising by the bay.
I did not watch where you might come,
For you had never been away.
For you have never been away.

Charles Causley

'The Last Rejoicing'

In November came Guy Fawkes Day, a flash of brightness, when we lighted our great bonfire in the ploughfield and sent our rockets curving to the night sky. Catherine-wheels whizzed, pinned on the stable door in the time-honoured place, and jump-jacks leapt like live things across the yard to the barn. We saw the flares of distant fires, and we heard the bang of a cannon. We roasted our potatoes in the ashes of our fire, and ate the floury meal of them. We had parkin for supper, and bonfire toffee under the stars. It was a pagan feast in the midst of the hills, and a wonderful day for a birthday. That was the last rejoicing till December came.

Alison Uttley
from Country Hoard

Fireworks

They rise like sudden fiery flowers,
    They burst upon the night,
Then fall to earth in burning showers
    Of crimson, blue and white.

Like buds too wonderful to name,
    Each miracle unfolds,
And catherine-wheels begin to flame
    Like whirling marigolds.

Rockets and Roman candles make
    An orchard of the sky,
When magic trees their petals shake
    Upon each gazing eye.

James Reeves

'St Martin's Summer'

When Jane woke on the first day of November the walls of her room were glowing rosy red. The window was open a little and as the sun crept up the fiery sky Jane smelled the lovely scent of bonfire smoke. She remembered her uncle lighting the fire two evenings ago. It had burned slowly ever since. When she got back from school yesterday she had run out into the garden and watched the thin plume of blue smoke rising into the misty dusk. Now she slipped her fingers from under the bedclothes, held them to her little freckled nose and sniffed hard. She could smell smoke but was not sure whether it came from her hands or not. She liked the smell anyhow and oddly enough, it was almost the only country smell that reminded her of home, for a bonfire smells the same wherever it burns, though never so sharply sweet as on an October or November evening. She moved her hands behind her head again and watched the glow of the rising sun on the beamed ceiling. She remembered how her father came home from work for lunch on Saturday and then, as quickly as he could, changed into his old clothes and went to work in the garden. And in the autumn all the little gardens in their road would have a bonfire burning on Saturday and Sunday afternoons. . . .

The frost held for two more days and then broke suddenly and the next Saturday was bright and warm. 'St Martin's summer, Martinmas,' Mrs Watson said. ''Tis often the same round about mid-November.'

As Jane plodded through the carpet of mucky straw

to cross the rickyard, she smacked a frisky young Red Poll on her behind and made her move. The dogs were already exploring the hedge at the side of the field when she and her uncle climbed the locked gate and looked down the hill to see the first faint blue-green tinge of the wheat sown only a few weeks ago. Thousands upon thousands of rows of neat little blades were already pushing through the brown soil and Jane remembered how she had walked through the stubble not long ago and seen a few flowers still blooming. A great flock of birds flew up from the hedgerow which was bright with scarlet haws. Presently on another field she saw the fieldfares which were bigger than the redwings. Out in the sheep field old Frank was already getting ready to build his lambing pens.

And so November slipped by. St Martin's summer was short-lived and Mrs Watson had been wise to warn Jane to make the best of it, for after but three more days the rain came and never seemed to stop. Day after day her uncle used the car to take Jane to and from school. The lanes were slippery with dead and fallen leaves, and all the country smelled of damp decay. Shorter and shorter were the hours of daylight as the year prepared to die and Jane grew to love the welcome of firelight and lamplight as she rushed down the hill in the old car on each afternoon.

Malcolm Saville
from Jane's Country Year

The brief patch of warmth in mid-November is named after the soldier saint whose feast is celebrated on November 11. St Martin sliced his warm army cloak in two, and gave half to a shivering beggar. That night he had a dream in which he saw Christ wrapped in the half-cloak, and this led to his conversion. The gleam of November sun recalls his generosity.

Digging

To-day I think
Only with scents, – scents dead leaves yield,
And bracken, and wild carrot's seed,
And the square mustard field;

Odours that rise
When the spade wounds the root of tree,
Rose, currant, raspberry, or goutweed,
Rhubarb or celery;

The smoke's smell, too,
Flowing from where a bonfire burns
The dead, the waste, the dangerous,
And all to sweetness turns.

It is enough
To smell, to crumble the dark earth,
While the robin sings over again
Sad songs of Autumn mirth.

Edward Thomas

Autumn

I love the fitful gust that shakes
   The casement all the day,
And from the mossy elm-tree takes
   The faded leaf away,
Twirling it by the window-pane
With thousand others down the lane.

I love to see the shaking twig
   Dance till the shut of eve,
The sparrow on the cottage rig,
   Whose chirp would make believe
That spring was just now flirting by
In summer's lap with flowers to lie.

I love to see the cottage smoke
   Curl upwards through the trees;
The pigeons nestled round the cote
   On November days like these;
The cock upon the dunghill crowing,
The mill-sails on the heath a-going. . . .

John Clare

November

November's days are thirty:
November's earth is dirty,
Those thirty days, from first to last;
And the prettiest things on ground are the paths
With morning and evening hobnails dinted,
With foot and wing-tip overprinted
Or separately charactered,
Of little beast and little bird.
The fields are mashed by sheep, the roads
Make the worst going, the best the woods
Where dead leaves upward and downward scatter.
Few care for the mixture of earth and water,
Twig, leaf, flint, thorn,
Straw, feather, all that men scorn,
Pounded up and sodden by flood,
Condemned as mud.

But of all the months when earth is greener
Not one has clean skies that are cleaner.
Clean and clear and sweet and cold,
They shine above the earth so old,
While the after-tempest cloud
Sails over in silence though winds are loud,
Till the full moon in the east
Looks at the planet in the west
And earth is silent as it is black,
Yet not unhappy for its lack.
Up from the dirty earth men stare:
One imagines a refuge there
Above the mud, in the pure bright
Of the cloudless heavenly light:

Another loves earth and November more dearly
Because without them, he sees clearly,
The sky would be nothing more to his eye
Than he, in any case, is to the sky;
He loves even the mud whose dyes
Renounce all brightness to the skies.

Edward Thomas

'Fall, Leaves, Fall'

Fall, leaves, fall; die, flowers, away;
Lengthen night and shorten day;
Every leaf speaks bliss to me
Fluttering from the autumn tree.
I shall smile when wreaths of snow
Blossom where the rose should grow;
I shall sing when night's decay
Ushers in a drearier day.

Emily Brontë

Summer is Gone

My tidings for you: the stag bells,
Winter snows, summer is gone.
Wind high and cold, low the sun
Short his course, sea running high.

Deep-red the bracken, its shape all gone –
The wild-goose has raised his wonted cry;
Cold has caught the wings of birds;
Season of ice – these are my tidings.

translated by Kuno Meyer
from a Celtic poem

Winter
Reflections

He giveth snow like wool:
He scattereth the hoarfrost like ashes.
He casteth forth his ice like morsels:
Who can stand before his cold?

What a wealth of unforgettable prose and verse is offered to us by writers and poets for the passing of the year. The more I searched, the more difficult it became to make a final choice, until I realised, as I hope you will do, that the transition of winter is not an end. It is a rebirth, because at its very core is the greatest story of all time.

The first Christmas is not just a sentimental story of a new-born baby crying in the winter night, but a challenge to mankind, and a promise of hope and comfort. I had to include this incomparably told story again, and have also chosen another beautiful piece of writing by Laurie Lee, describing a Christmas in the English countryside when he was young.

I hope you will like *An Appreciation of Grandmothers* which was found in the parish magazine of a church in the East End of London. This was one of my luckiest discoveries. *Alone in the Town* was written by my eldest grandson when he was still at school, and seems to express the loneliness of adolescence, but there is much else which is as mature as the passing of the year.

Then, after the miracle of Christmas, follow yet another forty days in the Christian calendar, until the festival of Candlemas is celebrated on the second day of February. And so, before the first snowdrops herald another Spring, I offer you a Robert Herrick poem, followed by the lovely verses of the modern poet, Charles Causley. Finally, as Mary Webb reminds us, in the last line, of the last verse, of the last poem, in this journey through the seasons –

'And Spring awakes and laughs across the snow'.

. . . Ah, bitter chill it was!
The owl, for all his feathers, was a-cold;
The hare limped trembling through the frozen grass,
And silent was the flock in woolly fold.

John Keats

Winter

The frost is here,
And fuel is dear, ·
And woods are sear,
And the fire burns clear,
And frost is here
And has bitten the heel of the going year.

Bite, frost, bite!
You roll away from the light
The blue wood-louse and the plump dormouse,
And the bees are stilled and the flies are killed,
And you bite far into the heart of the house,
But not into mine.

Bite, frost, bite!
The woods are all the searer,
The fuel is all the dearer,
The fires are all the clearer,
The spring is all the nearer,
You have bitten into the heart of the earth,
But not into mine.

Alfred, Lord Tennyson

The Bullfinch

I saw upon a winter's day
A bullfinch on a hedgerow spray;
He piped one note.
And since the countryside was mute,
As pure as rain I heard the flute
Of that small throat.

He picked a rotting willow-seed;
He whistled, in his joy to feed,
A whole sweet stave.
His sloe-black head, how shining sleek,
How strong his blunted, sooty beak,
His eye, how brave!

Then boldly down he came to drink
Out of a roadside puddle's brink,
Half ice, half mud;
So coral-breasted, sturdy, merry,
That I forgave him plum and cherry
Nipped in the bud.

Betty Hughes

Alone in the Town

All is quiet,
Silence shrouds the sleeping
Hub of civilisation,
I am alone and it is winter.

Darkness envelops us
Silently,
Slipping into unknown, unwalked
Alleys of years forgotten.

I hear the dangling conversation of
The river,
And the heron who knows me.

It is raining
Softly,
And I am alone.
I have solitude and
I am solitary,
In the town of my beginning.

James Mettyear

Snow

No breath of wind,
No gleam of sun –
Still the white snow
Whirls softly down –
Twig and bough
And blade and thorn
All in an icy
Quiet, forlorn.
Whispering, rustling,
Through the air,
On sill and stone,
Roof – everywhere,
It heaps its powdery
Crystal flakes,
Of every tree
A mountain makes;
Till pale and faint
At shut of day,
Stoops from the West
One wintry ray.
And, feathered in fire,
Where ghosts the moon,
A robin shrills
His lonely tune.

Walter de la Mare

Snow

In the gloom of whiteness,
In the great silence of snow,
A child was sighing
And bitterly saying: 'Oh,
They have killed a white bird up there on her nest,
The down is fluttering from her breast!'
And still it fell through that dusky brightness
On the child crying for the bird of the snow.

Edward Thomas

The Warm and the Cold

Freezing dusk is closing
  Like a slow trap of steel
On trees and roads and hills and all
  That can no longer feel.
    But the carp is in its depth
      Like a planet in its heaven.
    And the badger in its bedding
      Like a loaf in the oven.
    And the butterfly in its mummy
      Like a viol in its case.
    And the owl in its feathers
      Like a doll in its lace.

Freezing dusk has tightened
  Like a nut screwed tight
On the starry aeroplane
  Of the soaring night.
      But the trout is in its hole
        Like a chuckle in a sleeper.
      The hare strays down the highway
        Like a root going deeper.
      The snail is dry in the outhouse
        Like a seed in a sunflower.
      The owl is pale on the gatepost
        Like a clock on its tower.

Moonlight freezes the shaggy world
  Like a mammoth of ice –
The past and the future
  Are the jaws of a steel vice.
      But the cod is in the tide-rip
        Like a key in a purse.
      The deer are on the bare-blown hill
        Like smiles on a nurse.
      The flies are behind the plaster
        Like the lost score of a jig.
      Sparrows are in the ivy-clump
        Like money in a pig.

Such a frost
  The flimsy moon
    Has lost her wits.

      A star falls.

The sweating farmers
  Turn in their sleep
    Like oxen on spits.

Ted Hughes

Stopping by Woods on a Snowy Evening

Whose woods these are I think I know.
His house is in the village though;
He will not see me stopping here
To watch his woods fill up with snow.

My little horse must think it queer
To stop without a farmhouse near
Between the woods and frozen lake
The darkest evening of the year.

He gives his harness bells a shake
To ask if there is some mistake.
The only other sound's the sweep
Of easy wind and downy flake.

The woods are lovely, dark and deep,
But I have promises to keep,
And miles to go before I sleep,
And miles to go before I sleep.

Robert Frost

'When Icicles Hang by the Wall'

When icicles hang by the wall,
   And Dick the shepherd blows his nail,
And Tom bears logs into the hall,
   And milk comes frozen home in pail,
When blood is nipp'd and ways be foul,
   Then nightly sings the staring owl,
         Tu-whit,
   To-who, a merry note,
While greasy Joan doth keel the pot.

When all aloud the wind doth blow,
   And coughing drowns the parson's saw,
And birds sit brooding in the snow,
   And Marian's nose looks red and raw,
When roasted crabs hiss in the bowl,
   Then nightly sings the staring owl,
         Tu-whit,
   Tu-who, a merry note,
While greasy Joan doth keel the pot.

William Shakespeare

Forty Days of Christmas

Make we mirth
For Christ's birth,
And sing we Yule to Candlemas.

December 25 *Christmas* *Day*	The first day of Yule we have in mind How God was born man of our kind For he the bonds would now unbind Of all our sins and wickedness.
December 26 *St Stephen's* *Day*	The second day we sing of Stephen That slain with stones did rise up even To God whom he saw stand in heaven And there crowned was for his prowess.
December 27 *St John's* *Day*	The third day calls to mind St John Who was Christ's darling, dearer none, To whom Christ gave, when he was gone, His mother dear for her cleanness.
December 28 *Holy* *Innocents'* *Day*	The fourth day names the children young That Herod put to death with wrong And Christ they could not name with tongue But with their blood bore him witness.
December 29 *St Thomas of* *Canterbury's* *Day*	The fifth day brings in mind St Thomas That as a mighty pillar of brass Upheld the Church, and slain he was Because he stood for righteousness.

January 1
New
Year's
Day

The eighth day Jesus took his name
That saved mankind from sin and shame,
And circumcised was, not for blame
But for·to show his meekness.

January 6
Epiphany

The twelfth day offered him kings three
Gold, myrrh and incense, their gifts free,
For king and man and God was he,
Thus worshipped they his worthiness.

February 2
Candlemas

On the fortieth day came Mary mild
Unto the temple with her child
To be purified though undefiled,
And therewith endeth Christmas.

So make we mirth
For Christ's birth
And sing we Yule to Candlemas.

Thresholds

So here is come the night of nights!
On every pine a star is kindled.
Too slowly cumbrous summer dwindled;
But now the frostly silence hums
And comfort in the boundless darkness comes
  Along the heights.

Through weary times of brooding harm
We waited. Now the hour is ringing.
In haste we leave the wicket swinging
And whisper, splashing through the mire,
Of music and of colours bright like fire
  At Thresholds Farm.

Up yonder on the hill-side stark
The long sheds crouch beneath the larches.
We smile to think the whole world marches
With us to where the shippen gleams
And flower-pale faces cluster, keen as dreams,
  Against the dark.

We hear the cow-chains lift and fall;
We almost feel the ageless splendour
Of Child and Mother, warm and tender;
We run and softly push the door . . .
The mice go shrieking down the lonely floor,
  The empty stall.

Mary Webb

The Oxen

Christmas Eve, and twelve of the clock,
  'Now they are all on their knees,'
An elder said as we sat in a flock
  By the embers in hearthside ease.

We pictured the meek mild creatures where
  They dwelt in their strawy pen,
Nor did it occur to one of us there
  To doubt they were kneeling then.

So fair a fancy few would weave
  In these years! Yet, I feel,
If someone said on Christmas Eve,
  'Come; see the oxen kneel

In the lonely barton by yonder coomb
  Our childhood used to know,'
I should go with him in the gloom,
  Hoping it might be so.

Thomas Hardy

Christmas-Tide

We approached our last house high up on the hill, the place of Joseph the farmer. For him we had chosen a special carol, which was about the other Joseph, so that we always felt that singing it added a spicy cheek to the night. The last stretch of country to reach his farm was perhaps the most difficult of all. In these rough bare lanes, open to all winds, sheep were buried and wagons lost. Huddled together, we tramped in one another's footsteps, powdered snow blew into our screwed-up eyes, the candles burnt low, some blew out altogether, and we talked loudly above the gale.

Crossing, at last, the frozen mill-stream – whose

wheel in summer still turned a barren mechanism – we climbed up to Joseph's farm. Sheltered by trees, warm on its bed of snow, it seemed always to be like this. As always it was late; as always it was our final call. The snow had a fine crust upon it, and the old trees sparkled like tinsel.

We grouped ourselves round the farmhouse porch. The sky cleared, the broad streams of stars ran down over the valley and away to Wales. On Slad's white slopes, seen through the black sticks of its woods, some red lamps still burned in the windows.

Everything was quiet; everywhere there was the faint crackling silence of the winter night. We started singing, and we were all moved by the words and the sudden trueness of our voices. Pure, very clear, and breathless we sang.

> 'As Joseph was a-walking
> He heard an angel sing;
> "This night shall be the birth-time
> Of Christ the Heavenly King.
>
> He neither shall be borned
> In housen nor in hall,
> Nor in a place of paradise
> But in an ox's stall . . ."'

And two thousand Christmasses became real to us then; the houses, the halls, the places of paradise had all been visited; the stars were bright to guide the Kings through the snow; and across the farmyard we could hear the beasts in their stalls. We were given roast apples and hot mince pies, in our nostrils were spices like myrrh, and in our wooden box as we headed back for the village, there were golden gifts for all.

Laurie Lee
from Cider with Rosie

The First Christmas Day

. . . All went to be enrolled, each to his own city. And Joseph also went up from Galilee, from the city of Nazareth, to Judea, to the city of David, which is called Bethlehem, because he was of the house and lineage of David, to be enrolled with Mary, his betrothed, who was with child. And while they were there, the time came for her to be delivered. And she gave birth to her first-born son and wrapped him in swaddling clothes, and laid him in a manger, because there was no place for them in the inn.

And in that region there were shepherds out in the fields, keeping watch over their flock by night. And an angel of the Lord appeared to them, and the glory of the Lord shone around them, and they were filled with fear. And the angel said to them, 'Be not afraid; for behold, I bring you good news of great joy which will come to all the people; for to you is born this day in the city of David a Saviour, who is Christ the Lord. And this will be a sign for you; you will find a babe wrapped in swaddling clothes and lying in a manger.' And suddenly there was with the angel a multitude of the heavenly host praising God and saying, 'Glory to God in the highest, and on earth peace among men with whom he is pleased!'

And when the angels went away from them into heaven, the shepherds said to one another, 'Let us go over to Bethlehem, and see this thing that has happened, which the Lord has made known to us.' And they went with haste, and found Mary and Joseph, and the babe lying in a manger.

St Luke, 2, 3–20

Carol

In the bleak midwinter
    Frosty wind made moan,
Earth stood hard as iron,
    Water like a stone;
Snow had fallen, snow on snow,
    Snow on snow,
In the bleak midwinter
    Long ago.

Our God, heaven cannot hold Him,
    Nor earth sustain;
Heaven and earth shall flee away
    When He comes to reign;
In the bleak midwinter
    A stable-place sufficed
The Lord God Almighty
    Jesus Christ.

What can I give Him,
    Poor as I am?
If I were a shepherd
    I would bring a lamb;
If I were a wise man
    I would do my part –
Yet what I can, I give Him,
    Give my heart.

from a carol by
Christina Rossetti

The Animals Carol

Christus natus est! the cock   Christ is born
Carols on the morning dark.

Quando? croaks the raven stiff   When?
Freezing on the broken cliff.

Hoc nocte, replies the crow   This night
Beating high above the snow.

Ubi? ubi? booms the ox   Where?
From its cavern in the rocks.

Bethlehem, then bleats the sheep   Bethlehem
Huddled on the winter steep.

Quomodo? the brown hare clicks,   How?
Chattering among the sticks.

Humiliter, the careful wren   Humbly
Thrills upon the cold hedge-stone.

Cur? cur? sounds the coot   Why?
By the iron river-root.

Propter homine, the thrush   For the sake of
Sings on the sharp holly-bush.   man

Cui? cui? rings the chough   To whom?
On the strong, sea-haunted bluff.

Mary! Mary! calls the lamb   Mary
From the quiet of the womb.

Praeterea ex quo? cries   Who else?
The woodpecker to pallid skies.

Joseph, breathes the heavy shire   Joseph
Warming in its own blood-fire

Ultime ex quo? the owl
Solemnly begins the call.

De Deo, the little stare
Whistles on the hardening air.

Pridem? pridem? the jack snipe
From the stiff grass starts to pipe.

Sic et non, answers the fox
Tiptoeing the bitter lough.

Quomodo hoc scire potest?
Boldly flutes the robin redbreast.

Illo in eandem, squeaks
The mouse within the barley-sack.

Quae sarcinae? asks the daw
Swaggering from head to claw.

Nulla res, replies the ass,
Bearing on its back the Cross.

Quantum pecuniae? shrills
The wandering gull about the hills.

Ne nummum quidem, the rook
Caws across the rigid brook.

Nulla resne? barks the dog
By the crumbling fire-log.

Nil nisi cor amans, the dove
Murmurs from its house of love.

Who above all?

Of God

Long ago?

Yes and no

How do I
know this?

By going there

What luggage?

None

How much
money?

Not a penny

Nothing at all?

Only a loving
heart

    Gloria in Excelsis! Then
    Man is God, and God is Man.

Charles Causley

The Holly and the Ivy

The holly and the ivy,
  When they are both full grown,
Of all the trees that are in the wood,
  The holly bears the crown.

  The rising of the sun
  And the running of the deer,
  The playing of the merry organ,
  Sweet singing in the choir.

The holly bears a blossom
  As white as the lily flower,
And Mary bore sweet Jesus Christ
  To be our sweet saviour.

The holly bears a berry
  As red as any blood,
And Mary bore sweet Jesus Christ
  To do poor sinners good.

The holly bears a prickle
  As sharp as any thorn,
And Mary bore sweet Jesus Christ
  On Christmas day in the morn.

The holly bears a bark
  As bitter as any gall,
And Mary bore sweet Jesus Christ
  For to redeem us all.

In Midwinter a Wood was

In midwinter a wood was
where the sand-coloured deer ran
through quietness.
It was a marvellous thing
to see those deer running.

Softer than ashes
snow lay all winter where they ran,
and in the wood a holly tree was.
God, it was a marvellous thing
to see the deer running.

Between lime trunks grey or green
branch-headed stags went by
silently trotting.
A holly tree dark and crimson
sprouted at the wood's centre, thick and high
without a whisper, no other berry so fine.

Outside the wood was black midwinter,
over the downs that reared so solemn
wind rushed in gales, and strong here
wrapped around wood and holly fire
(where deer among the close limes ran)
with a storming circle of its thunder.
Under the trees it was a marvellous thing
to see the deer running.

Peter Levi

Keeping Christmas

Are you willing to forget what you have done for other people, and to remember what other people have done for you; to ignore what the world owes you, and to think what you owe the world; to put your rights in the background and your duties in the middle distance and your chances to do a little more than your duty in the foreground; to see that your fellow men are just as real as you are, and to try to look behind their faces to their hearts, hungry for joy; to own that probably the only good reason for your existence is not what you are doing to get out of life, but what you are doing to give to life; to close your book of complaints against the management of the universe and to look around you for a place where you can sow a few seeds of happiness – are you willing to do these things even for a day? Then you can keep Christmas.

Henry van Dyke

'A Wonderful Pudding'

There never was such a goose. Bob said he didn't believe there ever was such a goose cooked. Its tenderness and flavour, size and cheapness, were the themes of universal admiration. Eked out by the apple sauce and mashed potatoes, it was a sufficient dinner for the whole family; indeed, as Mrs Cratchit said with great delight (surveying one small atom of bone upon the dish), they hadn't ate it all at last! Yet everyone had had enough, and the youngest Cratchits in particular were steeped in sage and onion to the eyebrows! But now, the plates being changed by Miss Belinda, Mrs Cratchit left the room alone – too nervous to bear witnesses – to take the pudding up and bring it in. Suppose it should not be done enough! Suppose it should break in turning out! Suppose somebody should have got over the wall of the backyard, and stolen it, while they were merry with the goose – a supposition at which the two young Cratchits became livid! All sorts of horrors were supposed.

Hallo! A great deal of steam! The pudding was out of the copper. A smell like a washing-day! That was the cloth. A smell like an eating-house and a pastrycook's next door to each other, with a laundress's next door to that! That was the pudding! In half a minute Mrs Cratchit entered – flushed, but smiling proudly – with the pudding, like a speckled cannon-ball, so hard and firm, blazing in half of half-a-quarter of ignited brandy, and bedight with Christmas holly stuck into the top. Oh, a wonderful pudding! Bob Cratchit said, and calmly too, that he regarded it as the greatest success achieved by Mrs Cratchit since their marriage. Mrs Cratchit said that now the weight was off her mind, she would confess she had had her doubts about the quantity of flour. Everybody had something to say about it, but nobody said or thought it was at all a small pudding for a large family. It would have been flat heresy to do so. Any Cratchit would have blushed to hint at such a thing.

Charles Dickens
from A Christmas Carol

'A Holy Time'

In sum, it is a holy time, a duty in Christians for the remembrance of Christ, and a custom among friends for the maintenance of good fellowship. In brief, I thus conclude of it: I hold it a memory of the Heaven's love and the world's peace, the mirth of the honest and the meeting of the friendly.

Nicholas Breton
from Fantastickes

'Glad Christmas'

Neighbours resume their annual cheer
   Wishing, with smiles and spirits high,
Glad Christmas and a happy year
   To every morning passer-by;
Milkmaids their Christmas journeys go
   Accompanied with favour'd swain;
And children pace the crumping snow
   To taste their granny's cake again . . .

The yule cake dotted thick with plums
   Is on each supper table found,
And cats look up for falling crumbs
   Which greedy children litter round:
And housewife's sage-stuff'd season'd chine
   Long hung in chimney nook to dry,
And boiling elderberry wine
   To drink the Christmas eve's goodbye.

John Clare
from The Shepherd's Calendar

The Christmas Tree

At last there is the tree. . . . Suppose then, it has been reserved for this evening, decorated and kept behind locked doors for this hour. When the children enter that room it is already alight, and all other lights are extinguished; found there like a presence already arrived and serenely awaiting them, patient in splendour, becalming at first, or almost hypnotic, it needs only to be looked at. Even to older eyes it seems to be more than it is, more than a conifer covered with objects of metal and glass and wax, this image of a tree whose buds are flames, flowering at midwinter, a tree burning and unconsumed, evocative of the flourishing bay tree, and the burning bush, of the mystical 'Dream of the Rood', the Tree of Calvary itself, whose shadow is faint but indelible across the lights of the Nativity.

Laurence Whistler

New Year's Day : January 1

The old year now away is fled,
The new year it is entered:
Then let us now our sins down-tread,
And joyfully all appear –

God send you a happy New Year!

And now the New Year's gifts each friend
Unto each other they do send:
God grant we may all our lives amend,
And that the Truth may appear –

God send us a happy New Year!

The New Year's Gift

Let others look for pearl and gold,
Tissues or tabbies manifold;
One only look of that sweet hay
Whereon the blessed Baby lay,
Or one poor swaddling-clout, shall be
The richest New Year's gift to me.

Robert Herrick

For the last two or three hundred years, people have given
one another presents on Christmas Day; but in earlier times,
it was the custom to give them at New Year, remembering
the gifts that the three Magi gave to Jesus at Bethlehem. Their
adoration of Jesus is celebrated at Epiphany – January 6.

172

'Three Kings'

The Three Kings rode through the gate and the guard,
    Through the silent street, till their horses turned
And neighed as they entered the great inn-yard;
But the windows were closed,
    and the doors were barred,
    And only a light in the stable burned.

And cradled there in the scented hay,
    In the air made sweet by the breath of kine,
The little child in the manger lay,
The child that would be King one day
    Of a kingdom not human but divine.

His mother, Mary of Nazareth,
    Sat watching beside his place of rest,
Watching the even flow of his breath,
For the joy of life and the terror of death
    Were mingled together in her breast.

They laid their offerings at his feet:
    The gold was their tribute to a King,
The frankincense, with its odour sweet,
Was for the Priest, the Paraclete,
    The myrrh for the body's burying.

And the mother wondered and bowed her head,
    And sat as still as a statue of stone;
Her heart was troubled yet comforted,
Remembering what the Angel had said,
    Of an endless reign and of David's throne.

Henry Wadsworth Longfellow
from Three Kings Came Riding

Self-Pity

I never saw a wild thing
sorry for itself.
A small bird will drop frozen dead from a bough
without ever having felt sorry for itself.

D. H. Lawrence

Frost at Midnight

Therefore all seasons shall be sweet to thee,
Whether the summer clothe the general earth
With greenness, or the redbreast sit and sing
Betwixt the tufts of snow on the bare branch
Of mossy apple-tree, while the nigh thatch
Smokes in the sun-thaw; whether the eave-drops fall
Heard only in the trances of the blast,
Or if the secret ministry of frost
Shall hang them up in silent icicles,
Quietly shining to the quiet Moon.

Samuel Taylor Coleridge

This is part of a poem in which Coleridge is speaking to his
sleeping child, which lies in a cradle beside him, on a calm and
frosty night.

Never

'Does everybody have to die?' asked Kezia.

'Everybody!'

'Me?' Kezia sounded fearfully incredulous.

'Some day, my darling.'

'But, grandma.' Kezia waved her left leg and waggled the toes. They felt sandy. 'What if I just won't?'

The old woman sighed again and drew a long thread from the ball.

'We're not asked, Kezia,' she said sadly. 'It happens to all of us sooner or later.'

Kezia lay still, thinking this over. She didn't want to die. It meant she would have to leave here, leave every-where, for ever, leave – leave grandma. She rolled over quickly.

'Grandma,' she said in a startled voice.

'What, my pet!'

'You're not to die.' Kezia was very decided.

'Ah, Kezia' – her grandma looked up and smiled and shook her head – 'don't let's talk about it.'

'But you're not to. You couldn't leave me. You couldn't not be there.' This was awful. 'Promise me you won't ever do it, grandma,' pleaded Kezia.

The old woman went on knitting.

'Promise me! Say never!'

But still her grandma was silent.

Kezia rolled off the bed; she couldn't bear it any longer, and lightly she leapt on to her grandma's knees, clasped her hands round the old woman's throat and began kissing her under the chin, behind the ear, and blowing down her neck.

'Say never . . . say never . . . say never –' she gasped

between the kisses. And then she began, very softly and lightly, to tickle her grandma.

'Kezia!' The old woman dropped her knitting. She swung back in the rocker. She began to tickle Kezia. 'Say never, say never, say never,' gurgled Kezia, while they lay there laughing in each other's arms.

'Come, that's enough, my squirrel! That's enough, my wild pony!' said old Mrs Fairfield, setting her cap straight. 'Pick up my knitting.'

Both of them had forgotten what the 'never' was about.

Katherine Mansfield
from The Garden Party

An Appreciation of Grandmothers

A grandmother is a woman who has no children of her own so she loves the boys and girls of other people.

Grandmothers have nothing to do, they only have to be there. If they take you for a walk, they go slowly past beautiful things like leaves and caterpillars.

They never say, 'Come on quickly' or 'Hurry up for goodness' sake'. They are usually fat, but not too fat to tie up shoelaces.

They wear spectacles and sometimes take out their teeth. They can answer every question, for instance why dogs hate cats and why God isn't married. When they read to us they don't leave out anything. They do not mind if it's always the same story.

Everyone should have a Grandmother, especially those who have no television. Grandmothers are the only grown-ups who always have time.

A Summing Up

I have lived and I have loved;
I have waked and I have slept;
I have sung and I have danced;
I have smiled and I have wept;
I have won and wasted treasure;
I have had my fill of pleasure;
And all these things were weariness,
And some of them were dreariness,
And all these things, but two things,
Were emptiness and pain:
And Love – it was the best of them;
And Sleep – worth all the rest of them.

Charles Mackay

'Fear No More the Heat o' the Sun'

Fear no more the heat o' the sun,
   Nor the furious winter's rages;
Thou thy worldly task hast done,
   Home art gone, and ta'en thy wages.
Golden lads and girls all must,
As chimney-sweepers, come to dust.

Fear no more the frown o' the great,
   Thou art past the tyrant's stroke;
Care no more to clothe and eat,
   To thee the reed is as the oak.
The sceptre, learning, physic, must
All follow this, and come to dust.

Fear no more the lightning-flash,
   Nor the all-dreaded thunder-stone;
Fear not slander, censure rash;
   Thou hast finish'd joy and moan.
All lovers young, all lovers must
Consign to thee, and come to dust.

William Shakespeare

'And All the Trumpets Sounded'

After this it was noised abroad that Mr Valiant-for-Truth was taken with a Summons by the same Post as the other, and had this for a Token that the Summons was true, That his Pitcher was broken at the Fountain. When he understood it he called for his Friends, and told them of it. Then said he, 'I am going to my Father's, and tho' with great difficulty I am got hither, yet now I do not repent me of all the Trouble I have been at to arrive where I am. My Sword I give to him that shall succeed me in my Pilgrimage, and my Courage and Skill to him that can get it. My Marks and Scars I carry with me, to be a witness for me that I have fought his Battles who now will be my Rewarder.' When the day that he must go hence was come, many accompanied him to the River-side, into which as he went he said, 'Death, where is thy Sting?' And as he went down deeper he said, 'Grave, where is thy Victory?' So he passed over, and all the Trumpets sounded for him on the other side.

John Bunyan
from Pilgrim's Progress

Candlemas Eve

Down with the rosemary and bays,
    Down with the mistletoe;
Instead of holly, now upraise
    The greener box, for show.

The holly hitherto did sway:
    Let box now domineer
Until the dancing Easter day,
    Or Easter's eve appear.

Then youthful box, which now hath grace
    Your houses to renew,
Grown old, surrender must his place
    Unto the crispèd yew.

When yew is out, then birch comes in,
    And many flowers beside,
Both of a fresh and fragrant kin,
    To honour Whitsuntide.

Green rushes then, and sweetest bents,
    With cooler oaken boughs,
Come in for comely ornaments,
    To readorn the house.

Thus times do shift; each thing his turn does hold;
New things succeed, as former things grow old.

Robert Herrick

At Candlemas

'If Candlemas be fine and clear
There'll be two winters in that year';

But all the day the drumming sun
Brazened it out that spring had come,

And the tall elder on the scene
Unfolded the first leaves of green.

But when another morning came
With frost, as Candlemas with flame,

The sky was steel, there was no sun,
The elder leaves were dead and gone.

Out of a cold and crusted eye
The stiff pond stared up at the sky,

And on the scarcely breathing earth
A killing wind fell from the north;

But still within the elder tree
The strong sap rose, though none could see.

Charles Causley

Gathering Snowdrops

Froniga might call herself a Puritan, but the old religious customs, if they had anything to do with flowers, died hard in her, and on Candlemas day she went out to see if she could find any snowdrops, as her paternal grandmother and all her ancestresses had done for generations past. According to tradition the first snowdrops open on the second of February in memory of the Purification of our Lady and the Presentation of the Child Jesus in the temple, and in the days of faith were strewn upon every altar as emblems of purity.

'I'll find none this year,' thought Froniga, as she wrapped her cloak about her and went out into the garden. A partial thaw had melted most of the snow, but now it was bitterly cold again and wreaths of it still lay on the ground waiting for more snow to come and fetch it away. About the trunks of the apple trees, where the ground was mossy between the roots, the snowdrops always grew thickly in the spring, but now there were only leaves to be seen, there were no flowers. She went down to the far end of the orchard and pushed her way through the bushes to a sheltered dell in the copse beyond. Here she always found the first primroses and here she had planted snowdrop bulbs. She went down on her knees and searched among the wet leaves, and to her joy she found a few that were showing a little white. They had not yet learned humility and bent their heads, but were standing stiffly and uncompromisingly upright. They were shaped like spears, and like spears they would stand until their enemy the frost had relented a little and the warm air persuaded them to open their petals and bow to the sun.

Elizabeth Goudge
from The White Witch

The Snowdrop

Three softly curved white petals veined with light,
Three green-lined sepals, guarding frugal gold,
And all so strong to fold or to unfold!
Snow thunders from the bending pines. How slight
This frail, sheathed stem! Yet all unbent it springs,
So swift in stoopings and recoverings.

In the pale sunshine, with frail wings unfurled,
Comes to the bending snowdrop the first bee.
She gives her winter honey prudently;
And faint with travel in a bitter world,
The bee makes music, tentative and low,
And Spring awakes and laughs across the snow.

Mary Webb

Copyright Acknowledgments

e New Nutcracker Suite and Other Innocent Verses by Ogden Nash copyright 1961, 1962, by Ogden Nash.

Reprinted by permission of Miss Ivy Eastwick: 'Cherry Tree'.

Reprinted by permission of Harper & Row Publishers Inc. and World's ork Ltd: 'Sunning' from Crickety Cricket! by James S. Tippett (Text © pyright 1973 by Martha K. Tippett).

Reprinted by permission of Evans Brothers Ltd: 'Haytime' by Irene Paw- y from *The Book of a Thousand.Poems*.

Reprinted by permission of E. J. Scovell: 'Boy Fishing' from *The River eamer*, published by Barrie & Jenkins.

Reprinted by permission of Vallentine Mitchell Ltd, London: extracts from e *Diary of Anne Frank*.

Reprinted by permission of Macmillan Inc.: 'Something Told the Wild eese' by Rachel Field from *Branches Green*, © copyright 1934.

Reprinted by permission of The Hogarth Press: 'Second Chance' from *The rstborn* and 'Christmas-Tide' from *Cider with Rosie*, by Laurie Lee.

Reprinted by permission of Methuen & Co. Ltd: the quotation from *The ondon Year* by H. V. Morton.

Reprinted by permission of Hodder & Stoughton Ltd and David Higham ssociates Ltd: extracts from *Sister of the Angels* and *The White Witch* by lizabeth Goudge.

Reprinted by permission of Oxford University Press: 'Fireworks' from *he Blackbird in the Lilac* by James Reeves (1952).

Reprinted by permission of Constable Publishers: 'Summer is Gone' from our *Old Irish Songs of Summer and Winter* by Kuno Meyer.

Reprinted by permission of Mr James Mettyear: 'Alone in the Town'.

Reprinted by permission of Andre Deutsch Ltd: 'In Midwinter a Wood Was' from *The Gravel Ponds* by Peter Levi (1960).

Reprinted by permission of William Heinemann Ltd, Laurence Pollinger td, and the Estate of the late Mrs Frieda Lawrence: 'Self-Pity' from *The Complete Poems of D. H. Lawrence*. Reprinted by permission of William Heinemann Ltd: 'The Wind' from *The Wandering Moon* by James Reeves.

Reprinted by permission of Carousel (Transworld Publishers Ltd): extracts rom *Jane's Country Year* by Malcolm Saville.

The publishers would like to thank Mrs Myfanwy Thomas for permission o quote poems by her father Edward Thomas, from his *Collected Poems* ublished by Faber & Faber Ltd.

The poem *The Donkey* by Gertrude Hind was first published by *Punch*, to whom the publishers are grateful.

The compiler and the publishers regret that they have been unable to trace copyright-holders for *Lady Day* by G. James (first published by *Country Life*), *Two Sparrows* by Humbert Wolfe (first published by Ernest Benn Ltd in Kensington Gardens), and *A Country Calendar* by A. G. Street (published by Associated Book Publishers Ltd). They would welcome any information.

187

Index of Authors